Many of Tokyo's vegan eateries are small and tucked away, such as Chabuzen (see page 95).

THE VEGAN GUIDE TO TOKYO

東京のビーガンガイド

The ultimate guide to the best plant-based eats in Tokyo & beyond

CHIARA TERZUOLO

Smith Street Books

CONTENTS

INTRODUCTION
序説

When I first moved to Tokyo in 2011, I was a vegetarian foodie with high standards but almost no budget. Over the years, I was able to start eating out more regularly and began transitioning towards veganism, and my search for restaurants and stores that could supply high-quality and satisfying cruelty-free meals started to occupy a good deal of my time. However, vegan options were thin on the ground. Through trial and error (and carefully combing through Japanese blogs), I began to find hidden gems, and share them on Instagram at @tokyoveganguide.

It was not long before I started receiving messages from veggie folks desperate to visit Japan, but scared that in the land of sushi they wouldn't be able to eat anything besides white rice and steamed vegetables ... and so the first, self-published edition of the *Tokyo Vegan Guide* was born.

These days, the availability of plant-based cuisine in Tokyo has skyrocketed. Dozens of wonderful new restaurants have popped up across the city and interesting collaborations between non-vegan restaurants and plant-based chefs are becoming increasingly normal.

While still behind compared to most Western countries, it has become increasingly easy to find excellent vegan cuisine in Japan, partially thanks to the pre-COVID tourism boom.

This new edition – *The Vegan Guide to Tokyo* – is set to be the most comprehensive yet, and I hope it will make your travels easier, memorable and filled with delicious meals. Thank you for deciding to pick up this guide, and happy eating!

Chiara

A FEW QUIRKS ABOUT VEGANISM IN JAPAN

日本とビーガンの特徴

There are a few major cultural factors that explain why veganism is more prevalent in Japan than vegetarianism (although you may also notice the two terms are sometimes used interchangeably, which can be a bit confusing).

The first is historical, going back to pre–Meiji era Japan when raising and selling animals for consumption was banned, due to the strong Buddhist edicts of the time. The traditional Japanese diet, before the changes made to 'modernise' the country during the Meiji era, was mainly based on barley, rice, miso, veggies, occasional fish and more rarely still meat (used mainly for 'medicinal' purposes). We can still see echoes of this diet in *shojin ryori*, the cuisine of Buddhist monks, who in general also avoid eggs and pungent vegetables like garlic and onions.

As for milk products, these are still a relatively recent addition to the Japanese diet, first introduced during the Meiji era, when thinkers of the time believed that dairy and meat products would make the population stronger and more similar to the Europeans with whom they had started to trade and create political alliances. During the United States' occupation of Japan after World War II, the authorities pushed the use of milk products to boost protein consumption for children.

The other aspect that gives veganism a leg-up is the high prevalence of macrobiotic cuisine, a concept many visitors encounter for the first time. Many cafes and restaurants in Japan, including some in this guide, label themselves as macrobiotic rather than vegan. While it is a health regimen rather than an ethical choice, on the whole macrobiotic diets are just a short step away from veganism.

Popularised by George Ohsawa and Michio Kushi, macrobiotic diets in Japan usually revolve around locally grown produce, cereals, miso and beans, using little oil and mild seasonings. The occasional use of naturally raised fish and meat products means that macrobiotic cuisine is not necessarily completely plant-based; however, shops and restaurants that run on these principles will be more aware of your needs as a vegan.

NOTES ABOUT THIS GUIDE
ガイドに関して

Until quite recently in Japan, veganism was often considered a stoic, health-based choice, due to being confused with macrobiotic diets. However, over the past couple years there has been a boom of interest in reducing meat consumption, and an increasing understanding that vegan cuisine is not boring nor flavourless.

This is, of course, a major boon for plant-based foodies, as it means not just going out for another meal, but enjoying something that makes your eyes light up at the flavours dancing along your tongue. The eateries selected for this guide are those which provide (in my personal opinion) exactly that experience. My lifelong love of good food, excellent wine and proper presentation are not in one bit affected by my choice to live as cruelty-free an existence as possible.

When travelling, the experience of trying traditional dishes is one of the great pleasures of visiting a new country. While a few standout Western-style and Western-influenced joints have made the list, I have tried to give pride of place to restaurants which offer local cuisine, so that you can experience the flavours of Japan without having to compromise your beliefs.

Most of the cafes and restaurants included in this guide are 100 per cent vegan, for peace of mind and to allow for the thrill of having the whole menu to choose from. For the macrobiotic and omni restaurants, only those which are very clear about veganism, and which can be trusted to take your requests seriously, have been included.

Those already familiar with the city or the excellent HappyCow app may notice that not all of Tokyo's vegan restaurants are listed. No disrespect is meant to any of these establishments; in fact, a few of my personal favourites have not made the cut! My reasons for not including them are not necessarily due to the quality of the food on offer. Selections were made taking into consideration location, opening hours, uniqueness of the dishes served and the likelihood of survival in Tokyo's famously competitive restaurant scene.

Some areas with hidden vegan hotspots do not offer sights of great note. I understand that most visitors to Tokyo have limited time in the city and travelling 40–60 minutes just for a meal would be difficult. For this reason, I have tried to list as many restaurants as possible in areas where travellers are most likely to visit. You will also find some suggestions for popular day-trip destinations from Tokyo, along with some tips for the major tourist magnets of Kyoto and Osaka.

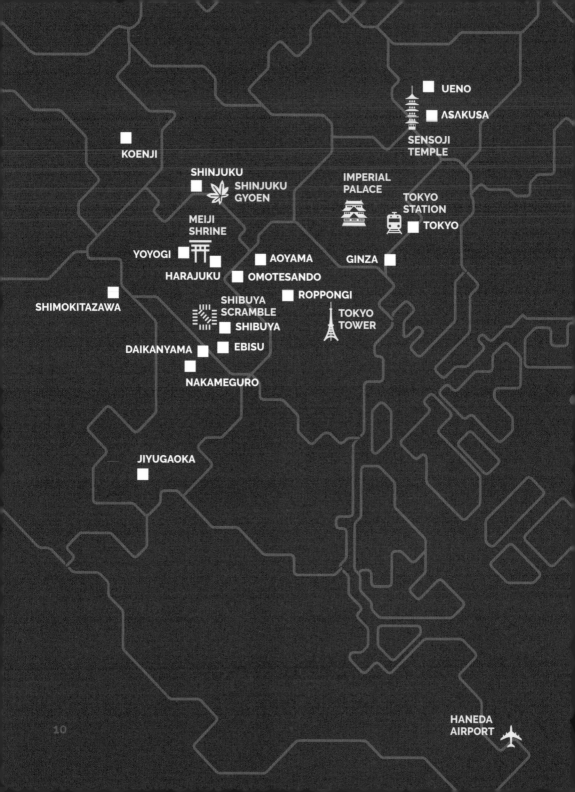

POPULAR TOKYO SUBURBS & MAJOR SIGHTSEEING SPOTS

人気観光スポット

TOKYO INNER WARDS

As one of the largest cities in the world, Tokyo can seem truly endless. Most visitors tend to stay within the major 23 wards, where you will also find the city's most famous sights. The majority of the restaurants in this section are located in areas close to popular sightseeing spots, so you can easily pop by while exploring.

Home to one of the city's largest and most confusing train and metro stations, Shinjuku is a central juncture, and where many of Tokyo's citizens come to shop in the numerous department stores, enjoy a night out or catch up with friends. One of the highlights of this area is Shinjuku Gyoen National Garden, a large park with fine Japanese gardens, beautiful *sakura* (cherry blossoms) in spring, red autumn leaves and centennial trees that provide a spectacular contrast to the towering skyscrapers on the horizon.

Not far from the park is the warren of bars known as Golden Gai. Some of these small drinking spots are very tourist friendly, and the little alleys hark back to Shinjuku's humble beginnings as an area for travellers and day labourers. Pop by the nearby shrine, Hanazono Jinja, which is nicely spooky at night.

A bit racier (but still quite safe for visitors), the streets of Kabukicho are filled with neon signs and huge posters advertising hostesses, hosts and other services that are probably best left untranslated. The popular Robot Restaurant, Samurai Museum and Godzilla statue are also found here.

LGBTQ+ visitors will want to visit the Ni-Chome area, home to Tokyo's largest concentration of queer spaces, with Arty Farty and AiiRO being two good spots to start your evening. A quick zip through Omoide Yokocho (Memory Alley) is sufficient, and if you want a good (and above all, free!) view of the city, head over to the Tokyo Metropolitan Government Building and ride the elevator all the way to the top.

SHINJUKU

新宿

ADDRESS

Shimura Building 4F,
2-5-8 Shinjuku,
Shinjuku-ku, Tokyo

HOW TO GET THERE

positioned next to Exit C5
of Shinjuku-Sanchome
Station. Look for the
Doutor coffee shop –
Kiboko is on the 4th
floor of the same
building (its windows are
decorated with hippos).

OPENING HOURS

Thursday–Saturday
from 18:00 to 23:00
(last order 21:00)

PRICE

2200 yen for the large
tapas plate required as
your 'seat fee'

Kiboko
キボコ

Kiboko (which means hippopotamus in Swahili) has
an enviable location right by Shinjuku Gyoen park and
the Shinjuku-Sanchome metro station. The owner/
chef does a remarkable job of dishing out yummy
wine-bar food and *izakaya* (Japanese pub) style fare
accompanied by bio wines.

Note that the owner currently requires all guests to
order the 10-dish tapas plate as a 'seat fee', which is an
unusual system but delicious nonetheless. If the tapas
aren't enough, the a la carte menu changes seasonally,
with a few standout dishes, such as the coriander-
stuffed *gyoza* potstickers and the complex and robust
trippa-style stew with a pleasing kick of tomato. In
winter, be sure to try the *oden* hotpot. The eggless
Spanish *tortilla* omelette is creamy and comforting,
perfect after a long day of walking around. Make sure
to leave space for the fruit tarts, which are imaginative
and filled with nutty goodness.

Top: The tapas plate lets you try a little bit of everything.

ADDRESS

Shinjuku Isetan Main Building 7F, 3-14-1 Shinjuku, Shinjuku-ku, Tokyo

HOW TO GET THERE

follow the signs in Shinjuku-Sanchome Station directing you to the Isetan department store (or find exits B3 or B4) and go up to the restaurant floor

OPENING HOURS

daily (except on days the department store is closed) from 11:00 to 22:00

PRICE

this is a relatively classy restaurant, located in an upscale department store. Expect to pay 2000–4000 yen for lunch and 4000–7000 yen for dinner, depending on menu choices.

Green Italian TORCIA

グリーン イタリアン トルチャ

Formerly known as Chaya Macrobiotics, this swanky spot is about as far away as you can get from the 'hippy' image of veganism. Elegant wood decor and lovely presentation of dishes are some of the drawing points of this newly renovated omni restaurant, making it a lovely stop for a special lunch or dinner with non-vegan friends.

The lunch course is an excellent deal at under 3000 yen, featuring seasonal croquettes, a truffle and *yuba* carbonara (that is well worth the additional fee) and hamburger 'steaks' with *demi-glace* sauce. If you go for dinner, the vegan *foie gras* with *ravigote* sauce is totally unique. The dessert menu is heavily vegan and is both beautiful and completely scrumptious. If you are on a budget, opt for a slice of cake or a patisserie and a cup of coffee as an afternoon treat. For a less expensive option, look up their Hibiya branch, which you can read about on page 45, in the Ginza section of this guide.

Top: Beautifully presented, Italian-inspired dishes are a specialty.
Bottom: The interesting desserts are just right for an afternoon tea break.

ADDRESS
Marui Main Building 5F,
3-30-13 Shinjuku,
Shinjuku-ku, Tokyo

⚓ HOW TO GET THERE
located inside the Marui
department store, which
is directly connected
to Shinjuku-Sanchome
Station via Exit A1, or is
just a short walk from
Exit A4

🕐 OPENING HOURS
Monday–Saturday from
11:00 to 21:00; Sundays
and public holidays
from 11:00 to 20:30
(last order 30 minutes
before closing)

Ⓨ PRICE
around 930–1380 yen
for a meal or a sundae;
630–980 yen for
vegan cakes

Futaba Fruits Parlor
フタバフルーツパーラー

Futaba Fruits is surprisingly cosy despite being housed inside a department store. While they do have a few decent food options, such as a simple curry and a tofu-based chilli, the main draw here is the dessert menu. If you have been drooling over Japanese fruit sandwiches, the kiwi, strawberry and mango version here is big enough to share. Their incredible stacked ice-cream parfaits can all be made vegan for an extra 100 yen, including the thick and satisfying whipped cream. The apple, cranberry and caramel version is particularly good – a celebration of autumn in a glass. Even their cream *anmitsu* (a dessert with agar jelly, fruit, red bean paste and black sugar syrup) can be veganised, in case you want to try a more traditional Japanese dessert. Vegan and gluten-free options are marked, but most of the text is Japanese so ask the friendly staff for a bit of help if you get confused.

Top: Try one of Futaba's famous Japanese fruit sandwiches.
Bottom: Besides desserts, there are a few simple savoury meals available.

ADDRESS

Shinjuku Q Building,
3-8-9 Shinjuku,
Shinjuku-ku, Tokyo

HOW TO GET THERE

positioned outside
Exit C5 of Shinjuku-
Sanchome Station

OPENING HOURS

Monday–Friday lunch
from 11:30 to 15:00; dinner
from 18:00 to 20:00.
Saturday–Sunday lunch
from 11:30 to 16:00; dinner
from 18:00 to 20:00.

PRICE

from 1800 yen for lunch;
budget at least 3000–
4000 yen for dinner

Ain Soph. Journey

アインソフジャーニー

Ain Soph offers simple, Western-style vegan food. It's best to visit for a weekday lunch, as on the weekends it can get crowded, and the prices are higher. A few highlights are the seasonal quiche – a comforting dish with a flaky puff-pastry crust – and the *hayashi* rice, a rich *demi-glace* stew that is a *yoshoku* (Japanese-style Western cuisine) classic. Leave some space for their seasonal desserts or crème brûlée. If you are looking for a brunch spot, the fluffy 'heavenly pancakes' live up to their name, and the Moroccan soy latte is a top-notch accompaniment.

*Top: Dreamy, fluffy vegan pancakes, anyone? **Bottom right:** A savoury plate of* hayashi *rice.*

Parkside Square 1F, 2-1-5 Shinjuku, Shinjuku-ku, Tokyo

HOW TO GET THERE

take a left from Exit 1 of Shinjuku-Gyoenmae Station and then turn into the next street on your left, walking all the way down until you reach the park. The cafe is also just a short walk from the main entrance of Shinjuku Gyoen.

OPENING HOURS

daily from 11:00 to 19:00

PRICE

most cakes around 700–800 yen

Marbre Vegan
マルブルヴィーガン

This tiny spot right by the lovely Shinjuku Gyoen National Garden mainly serves cakes and simple coffee drinks. Be sure to try the Japanese-style strawberry shortcake and popular blueberry tart, which have a richness indistinguishable from non-vegan desserts. They clearly write out all the ingredients of each cake, so this is also a good place for those who are gluten intolerant or need to be careful of food allergies. They sell a daily sandwich from Monday to Thursday, and on two Saturdays a month they offer two sandwich options. If you are lucky, you may visit on the two Fridays a month when they sell freshly made Japanese-style fruit sandos.

Top: Marbre vegan is a haven for visitors with a sweet tooth.

Tourists flock to the famous Scramble Crossing, while the younger crowd goes to Shibuya to party, usually meeting up in front of Hachiko, the famous statue of the dog who waited for her beloved but sadly departed owner in front of the station. During Halloween, this is the place to be seen, with the entire area shut off to traffic to allow for costumed revelry.

Shibuya has a plethora of shopping options (including the rather awesome Loft store), and a few smaller gems, such as Nombei Yokocho (a little street of bars, similar to Golden Gai in Shinjuku) and Dogenzaka (also known as Love Hotel Hill), where you can still see a few of the more over-the-top facades. This area is quite close to both Harajuku and Daikanyama, and taking a stroll through the smaller streets is a good opportunity to discover unusual fashion and even odder specialty stores. Art lovers should stop by the overhead pass of the Shibuya Mark City shopping/station building, where you can see the Japanese artist Taro Okamoto's huge mural 'The Myth of Tomorrow'. This is also a good spot to get a view of the Scramble Crossing without getting crushed. There are many vegan-friendly options in this area, so if none of the recommendations here fit the bill, a quick internet search will pull up alternative options.

The Yoyogi area is right next to Shibuya, and extends from Yoyogi Park all the way to Yoyogi-Uehara Station, several kilometres away. Most of the neighbourhood is residential, filled with designer homes, trendy restaurants and tiny expensive boutiques. Near Yoyogi-Uehara Station you can find the beautiful Tokyo Camii Mosque and Turkish Cultural Center, which is open daily for prayers and welcoming to visitors who wish to admire the lovely blue-and-white prayer hall.

This a good area for accommodation, as you get the benefit of being close to the major vegan hotspots of Harajuku/ Omotesando, Shibuya and Shinjuku, without the busyness.

SHIBUYA/
YOYOGI
渋谷・代々木

Izakaya Masaka
居酒屋 真さか

📍 **ADDRESS**
Shibuya Parco B1F,
15-1 Udagawacho,
Shibuya-ku, Tokyo

🛶 **HOW TO GET THERE**
from the Hachiko Exit of
Shibuya Station, cross the
Scramble to your right
onto Koen Dori street
(between the Starbucks
and Magnet buildings).
Go straight until the
street branches at the
MODI building. Take the
left branch and walk for
a couple of minutes until
you see the white Parco
department store.

🕐 **OPENING HOURS**
daily from 12:00 to 21:00
(last order 20:00)

¥ **PRICE**
around 1000–1200 yen
for lunch; budget 2000–
3000 yen for dinner

If you only eat one plate of vegan *karaage* (fried chicken) while in Japan, this is the place to do it. The completely unassuming little pub is tucked away in the basement of the Parco department store, surrounded by bright colours and other cool eateries. The decor is old school and minimal, which is fine because the star of the show here is the vegan Japanese soul food at affordable prices. If you are stopping by for lunch, go ahead and order the *karaage* set, which comes with rice, pickles, soup and your choice of sauce. The tartare and sesame chilli are particularly tasty, complementing the crispy crumb and juicy, satisfying 'meat' inside. In the evening be sure to try a range of side dishes, such as the delightfully retro pasta salad, crunchy *menma* bamboo shoots or the Manchurian cauliflower.

*Top: The hyper-realistic food samples in the window make choosing what to order easier. **Right**: Huge, juicy karaage smothered in your choice of sauce.*

ADDRESS

1-27-6, Higashi,
Shibuya-ku, Tokyo

HOW TO GET THERE

turn left out of the
New South Exit of
Shibuya Station onto
the large Meiji Dori main
road. Keep going straight
for about 5 minutes –
the restaurant will be
on the left, shortly
past the Namiki Bridge
intersection.

OPENING HOURS

Tuesday–Saturday lunch
from 11:30 to 16:00;
dinner from 17:30 to
21:00; Sunday, lunch only

PRICE

1200–1400 yen per bowl

Tsurushiko
麺ダイニングつるしこ

Most people have heard about ramen … but what about *reimen*? These firm, stretchy noodles are made from a combination of wheat and potato starch, and are one of the most famous dishes associated with the city of Morioka in Iwate Prefecture. Tsurushiko has taken this simple dish and reinvented it, and about half of their menu is vegan.

Reimen is available both cold and warm. On a cold day, the spicy warm noodles with *menma* bamboo shoots feels like a hug, while during the summer the avocado *reimen* in a creamy soup or Italian-inspired tomato and basil combo are soothing and refreshing. Not a soup fan? The soup-less sesame miso noodles with cucumber bites has a great kick of umami. Get a side dish of soy *karaage* for an extra bit of protein.

Top: The vegan options are both plentiful and prettily presented.
Bottom: Belly up to the counter and watch the chef work.

Nagi Shokudo
なぎ食堂

The oldest vegan restaurant in Shibuya, Nagi Shokudo has been serving local and visiting vegans, as well as people working nearby, for more than 10 years. The menu is built around three main set plates: a set of fried soy meat with a sauce; a curry set; and a set where you can choose three daily deli options. The fried soy meat, which I tried in both a chilli sauce and a Chinese chive sauce, is generously portioned. The curries are reliable, if not powerfully spiced, and the chocolate cake rounds things out nicely. In summer, try the *hiyajiru*, a chilled miso soup that is a specialty of Miyazaki Prefecture.

The interior is faded but not unwelcoming, but tall diners might struggle with the low chairs and tables. Lunch is better value than dinner.

⌖ ADDRESS
Royal Palace Shibuya 103, 15-10 Uguisudanicho, Shibuya-ku, Tokyo

⚓ HOW TO GET THERE
take a left out of the JR South Exit of Shibuya Station and climb the stairs to the pedestrian overpass. Walk across and go down the stairs, then keep walking to the left (passing the large guitar store) and take a right. Go straight up the hill and keep going until you see the Shibuya Sakuragaoka Post Office on your left. Right across the road in the basement of the building in front of you (under an Italian restaurant) you will find Nagi Shokudo. Look for the small red sign.

⏱ OPENING HOURS
Monday–Saturday lunch from 12:00 to 16:00 (last order 15:00); dinner from 18:00 to 23:00; Sunday, lunch only

ⓥ PRICE
1100–1500 yen for lunch sets; budget around 2500–3000 for dinner and a drink

Top: Stop by for a filling lunch of karaage *and fresh side dishes.*
Middle left: Pick up some snacks after your meal.

Hamanoya Parlor

はまの屋パーラー

Right next door to Izakaya Masaka, Hamanoya is the place to satisfy your desire to experience a retro Japanese *kissaten* (old-school coffee shop) without having to deal with stubborn owners who are likely to get snarky about veganising dishes. Sit at the counter, which looks like it came directly from the 1970s, and order one of the vegan *kissaten* specialties, along with an iced coffee. My go-to is the double curry topped with a crispy *katsu* cutlet. The combination of the fragrant smooth and dry curries coating the juicy cutlet is a match made in heaven. If you just want a quick snack, the *katsu* or 'egg' sandwiches are just right.

This is an omni spot, so be sure to request the vegan menu. After 17:30, it transforms into Campy! bar, perhaps the tiniest drag bar in Tokyo!

Top: Tuck into a tasty katsu *curry to refuel after exploring Shibuya.*

ADDRESS

2-6-16 Uehara, Shibuya-ku, Tokyo

HOW TO GET THERE

hidden away on a side street, this is a destination where having GPS will be helpful. From Yoyogi-Uehara Station, take either of the South exits and turn right. Keep walking straight until the road ends, and take a left. You should see the broad Inokashira Dori street in front of you. Cross the street and go left. Walk until the first street on your right (look for the green street lamps). Turn into this smaller street, and go straight, then take the first left into a small street. Follow it all the way down, and descend the stairs. Once you reach the road, take a left and walk straight for a few minutes. The restaurant will be on your right; look for the sign and white house.

OPENING HOURS

Wednesday–Sunday dinner only; starting times 19:00–21:00. Reserve at least a couple of days in advance through their website.

PRICE

8-course dinner is around 13,000 yen per person; wines start around 6000 yen per bottle

Tudore Tranquility

トゥドレ トランクイリティ

From the reservation process, where you are considerately asked if there are any foods you dislike, to the service and chance to chat with chef Mamta Reid, dining at Tudore Tranquility feels a bit like being invited to a dinner party at the home of a world-class chef, quickly followed by being transported to another planet. The two-hour meal flies by, one carefully prepared dish at a time. A recent menu included a robust pilaf of black quinoa, vegan parmesan and tarragon 'butter', an addictive curry-filled flatbread with spiced soy beans and palate cleansers of cashew mozzarella and ephemeral pineapple mousse, all rounded out by a platter of desserts so indulgent you are likely to be struck silent. It is quite a ride, and definitely a great spot for a romantic occasion. Do specify when reserving that you are vegan, as the standard courses are vegetarian, and feel free to ask the kind English-speaking staff any questions.

*Top: Inventive plant-based creations. **Bottom:** Let them know any preferences when booking, as they can accomodate most dietary needs.*

🧭 **HOW TO GET THERE**

from Yoyogi-Uehara Station, take either of the South exits and turn right. Keep walking straight until the road ends, and take a left. You should see the broad Inokashira Dori street in front of you. Cross the street and go left, following the large road. Walk for about 5 minutes, until the first street on your right (look for the green street lamps). Turn right into this smaller street, and go straight. Right after passing a small side street on your right, you should be able to see the sweet (candy) shop, recognisable by a small blue flag with a white circle flying from a pointy white building.

🕐 **OPENING HOURS**

Tuesday–Sunday from 10:30 to 18:00

💴 **PRICE**

around 300–500 yen for each sweet

Wa no Kashi Meguri

和のかし 巡

For fans of *wagashi* (Japanese sweets) or those curious to try them for the first time, Wanokashi is a 100 per cent vegan haven. Most of the sweets are also gluten free, with the exception of those that use soy sauce containing traces of wheat. They are most famous for their *fukumeguri daifuku*, soft rice cakes filled with agave-sweetened red and black bean paste. If you prefer something a little less bean-filled, the matcha cheesecake perfectly balances creaminess with the earthiness of high-quality green tea. Buy a few of the delightful *emikoboreruan*, literally 'smile-inducing sweets', which combine chocolate with matcha bean paste, pumpkin paste or other seasonal flavours, to take away.

Top: Get a taste of traditional Japanese sweets, such as dorayaki *(left) and* daifuku *(right).*

Strolling through Ginza is an opportunity to walk all over some of Japan's most expensive real estate, with certain spots going for 27 million yen per square metre! As such, it is not surprising that the broad walkways glitter with designer shops, busy department stores and lots of famous restaurants and bars. One of the best times to see the area is at sunset, as the signs flicker on and you can get a feeling for what this chic part of town must have been like during the 'Bubble Era' in the late 1980s. The side streets are equally interesting, with many high-class hostess bars and members-only clubs, with some buildings filled with them from top to toe.

Be sure to stop by the renovated Kabukiza Theatre, where you can often buy cheap 'one scene' tickets on performance days, to get a taste for this dramatic art in which performances can last several hours. A short walk away is what remains of Tsukiji Market and the Indian-inspired Tsukiji Honganji Temple.

Stationery fans will love both Itoya and Kyukyodo, where wonderful paper, writing utensils and notebooks await. The Ginza 5 mall has many tiny shops, including a few antique and kimono stores worth a browse, and the brand new Ginza Six is making waves.

For a matcha tea experience with a difference, Chanoha in the basement of the Matsuya department store is one of the most serene spots in the city. If you don't want to wait, they have excellent takeaway options (the green tea mixed with soda water being particularly good on a hot day). Right next door is a tiny sake bar, perfect for tasting a few cups of the country's famous rice wine. And beneath the tracks between Ginza and Tokyo stations you will find hundreds of small pubs and restaurants that, although not vegan, offer the chance to slip back in time to an older, less polished Tokyo.

GINZA

銀座

ADDRESS

Ginza Shochiku Square
1F, 1 -13-1 Tsukiji,
Chuo ku, Tokyo

HOW TO GET THERE

take Exit A2 at Higashi-
Ginza Station, and
immediately turn around
and walk towards the
Kabukiza Theatre by
crossing the large
intersection. Pass the
theatre, and keep
going until right after
a small urban park.
The restaurant is in the
large building on the left.

OPENING HOURS

daily from 7:00 to 21:00
(last order 20:30)

PRICE

1200–1500 yen for lunch;
2500–3500 yen for dinner
and drinks

Komeda IS
コメダイズ

The 100 per cent plant-based branch of the major Komeda coffee chain is a large airy place that offers a combination of *kissaten* (old-school Japanese coffee shop) classics, along with tapas-like dishes to mix and match for dinner with a glass of wine or fruit liqueur. Until 11:00 you can also experience a certified vegan version of the Japanese 'morning' breakfast sets so common at *kissaten*.

For lunch, the thick 'ham cutlet' or lemon-drizzled seared soy meat hot sandwiches are filling and pair well with a large oat milk latte. Another favourite is the creamy pasta gratin, or for a true only-in-Japan classic, try the the *napolitan*: a post-war creation of spaghetti in a tomato and ketchup-laced sauce with mushrooms, green peppers and (veggie) ham. On cold winter days go straight for the richness of the red wine–infused stew, with a few slices of baguette to mop up the sauce.

Note that the portions are large, so be careful of ordering too much, and leave room for dessert. The *shiro noir* is their most popular sweet treat, a Danish topped with almond milk soft-serve ice cream, or opt for the retro coffee jelly.

Bottom left: Katsu sandos are a popular kissaten treat.
Bottom right: Komeda IS is famous for its shiro noir pastry.

ADDRESS

Toho Hibiya Building B2F,
1-2-2 Yurakucho,
Chiyoda-ku, Tokyo

HOW TO GET THERE

from Exit A4 of Hibiya
Station, turn immediately
right, facing away from
the green overhead train
tracks. Walk straight
and take a left, right
before the pedestrian
crossing. Go past the
small Godzilla statue –
you should see the
large Chanter sign on a
building straight ahead.
The restaurant is on the
B2 floor of this building.

OPENING HOURS

daily from 11:00 to 22:00
(last order 21:00)

PRICE

1300–2500 yen for lunch;
2000–4000 yen for
dinner. Cakes are around
600 yen, and cake sets
cost 980 yen

Chaya Natural & Wild Table
チャヤ ナチュラル&ワイルドテーブル

A more casual branch of the macrobiotic Chaya group, this spot is hidden away in the basement of the Chanter department store. The food is served with practised reliability, and like Chaya's sister shops does serve some fish and meat. The fact that they serve food all day, and have both gluten-free and omni options, as well as their famous vegan cakes, make this is a reliable stand-by when checking out the Ginza/Hibiya area.

The simple but homely cuisine is *yoshoku* (Japanese versions of Western standards), with satisfying saucy 'hamburger steaks' and fresh deli plates that get swapped out seasonally. The Buddha bowl is packed with unusual veggies, and should leave you with just enough leeway to splurge and add a dessert for 440 yen. As Japan's most popular cake, the strawberry shortcake is a must-try and is not overly sweet, with lovely juicy berries taking pride of place. During dinner, a few additional entrees and set courses are available, with creative pasta and nicely presented appetisers giving extra flair.

Chaya also has a branch in Shiodome, near a number of large hotels. For a more elegant meal from this macrobiotic mainstay, check out Green Italian TORCIA in Shinjuku (see page 18).

Top: Opt for the veggie-filled Buddha bowl for a healthy energy boost.
Bottom right: Make sure you leave room for pudding!

Kyushu Jangara Ramen
九州じゃんがら 銀座店

📍 ADDRESS
6-12-17, Ginza, Chuo-ku, Tokyo

🦭 HOW TO GET THERE
take Exit A4 out of Ginza Station, then turn left at the first intersection. Keep going straight until you pass the Ginza Six building on your right. Cross the street and take another right; you should see the shop's bright blue, rainbow-decorated sign just ahead.

🕐 OPENING HOURS
daily from 11:00 to 22:00 (last order 21:45)

ⓨ PRICE
1000 yen for the vegan ramen; about 90–200 yen for various vegan toppings

Ginza restaurants can be pricey, so if you are on a budget this down-to-earth ramen joint will leave both you and your wallet full and happy. Lift Kyushu Jangara's bright *noren* curtain and step into the eclectic decor for a truly cheerful ramen experience. While most famous for their non-vegan *tonkotsu* ramen, this small chain offers one truly satisfying vegan bowl. Firm noodles float in an umami-rich soy sauce–based soup, to which you can add an additional kick by sprinkling in condiments like *shichimi* (hot pepper), milled garlic or sesame seeds. Toppings are simple, but the star of the show is their meat-free *chashu*. Usually made from braised pork, Jangara's version is created using layered tofu skin, called *yuba*, soaked in a delightfully savoury-sweet sauce, then lightly charred.

Besides Ginza, they also have branches in Akihabara, Kanda and Ikebukuro. Turn to page 52 for more on their main branch and restaurant, which has wider menu.

Top: Heaven is a big bowl of vegan ramen (with extra garlic!)

ADDRESS

Tokyo Ginza Shiseido Building 10F, 8-8-3, Ginza, Chuo-ku, Tokyo

HOW TO GET THERE

from Exit A2 of Ginza Station, walk straight ahead for about 7 minutes. Look for the striking red and gold building on your right.

OPENING HOURS

daily – lunch from 12:00 to 15:30 (last order 13:30); dinner from 18:00 to 23:00 (last order 20:00). Closed Sunday and Monday in mid-August and during New Year holidays. Reservations required.

PRICE

8000 yen for the lunch course; 15,000 yen for dinner (drinks not included)

Faro
ファロ

At the expensive end of the budget spectrum we have Faro, where Italian and Japanese gastronomy combine into edible art. Housed within the iconic deep-red Shiseido building, the cool blues and whites of the restaurant's interior create a feeling of being suspended in a cool ocean.

The ever-changing seasonal menu is definitely pricey, but worth the splurge for an unforgettable meal. Savoury mallow leaf panna cotta, handmade pastas that incorporate Japanese culinary sensibilities, a vegan cheese course, all rounded out by a spectacular flower tart … each new course is as pretty and surprising as the next.

The restaurant has earned a Michelin star and a Green Star for their sustainable practices. Be sure to make reservations well ahead of time, as in high season they are booked out two months in advance.

Bottom: Michelin-level vegan cuisine at its finest.

This area is one of Tokyo's major fashion hotspots, where visitors can see women in Lolita dress passing by gleaming designer shopfronts, and huge lines patiently waiting outside the most popular sweet (candy) shops *du jour*. This focus on fashion means that vegan-friendly joints are plentiful. After wandering around Cat Street, window shopping on Omotesando –considered the Champs-Élysées of Tokyo – and braving the brightly dressed teenagers on Takeshita Street, make sure to stroll through Meiji Shrine for a breath of fresh air, and maybe the opportunity to see a traditional Shinto wedding procession. The little Ota Museum is a charming spot, with an excellent collection of *ukiyoe* prints. Although a bit of a trek, the nearby Nezu Museum is also a must-see, with a fantastic Japanese-style garden and very photogenic tea houses.

Give yourself time to wander the back streets of Omotesando, which tend to be quieter, yet offer a plethora of interesting discoveries. This area has a particularly high number of vegan restaurants and cafes, so choosing a hotel nearby or with easy train connections may be a good idea to ensure you can check out as many as possible.

HARAJUKU/ OMOTESANDO/ AOYAMA

原宿・表参道・青山

HOW TO GET THERE

from the East Exit of
Harajuku Station or Exit 3
of Meiji-Jingumae Station,
turn onto Omotesando.
The two restaurants are
in the first building on
the left.

OPENING HOURS

Vegan Bistro Jangara –
daily from 11:00 to 22:00
(last order 21:30); Kyushu
Jangara Ramen – daily
from 10:00 to 22:00

PRICE

1080–1800 yen for lunch;
budget 2500–3000 for
dinner in order to try a
variety of dishes

Vegan Bistro Jangara & Kyushu Jangara Ramen

ヴィーガンビストロ じゃんがら&九州じゃんがら

If you have a hankering for a big bowl of ramen, on the first floor you can try two of Kyushu Jangara's signature bowls: the vegan *kumamoto*, a rich *tonkotsu* 'pork bone' broth topped with fried garlic, or the lighter vegan *shoyu*, a soy sauce–based soup.

For more varied options, take the elevator up to the second floor where you will find the green-painted bistro, with large windows overlooking the Omotesando shopping street. The star of the show here is the *juju* grill (or newly added *juju* hamburger), juicy soy meat served hot and sizzling on an iron plate. For an extra punch of umami, choose the miso sauce. You can also try a vegan version of *champon*, an iconic seafood and noodle dish from Nagasaki, along with some ramen options not available downstairs, such as *karabon* (a spicy, *tonkotsu*-style bowl). The gluten-free raspberry mousse cake and rather unusual 'shrub' drink are also well worth sampling.

Top: Enjoy views of Omotesando while enjoying a sizzling vegan hotplate at Vegan Bistro Jangara. *Bottom:* Ramen fans can get their fix at Kyushu Jangara Ramen downstairs.

5-1-8 Jingumae, Shibuya-ku, Tokyo

HOW TO GET THERE

take Exit A1 of Omotesando Station, then take the first left. It is the fifth building on your right.

OPENING HOURS

daily from 11:30 to 18:00 (last order 17:00)

PRICE

1500–1700 yen for lunch, with an extra 500 yen charge on weekends and public holidays

Brown Rice Canteen
ブラウンライス

Run by the Neal's Yard cosmetics company, the lunches at Brown Rice Canteen focus on simple, healthy ingredients presented in a beautiful, minimalist style. The daily lunch sets revolve around a main dish, often a tofu-based creation seasoned with miso, accompanied by rice, miso soup and two vegetable dishes (a traditional meal combination known as *ichiju sansai,* one soup and three sides). The steamed vegetable set is soothing, and the bean-based curry is quite mild with a nice balance of spices. The focus here is very Japanese in that the flavours of the vegetables are not tampered with, so don't expect fireworks. However, it leaves you feeling so virtuous that you'll have no qualms about sampling one of the rich, seasonal desserts. Just make sure to check the ingredients with the staff before you order, as occasionally they contain honey.

Top: Healthy daily sets feature tofu and other Japanese favourites.
Bottom: The serene interior matches the food perfectly.

Aoyama Takano
Building 2F, 3-5-4
Kitaaoyama, Minato-ku,
Tokyo

HOW TO GET THERE

from Exit A3 of
Omotesando Station,
walk straight and turn
left immediately onto
Aoyama Dori street
(right by the Sanyodo
bookshop). Walk straight
for a few minutes – the
Sincere Spa will be on
your left, a bit before the
pedestrian bridge. The
cafe is on the 2nd floor.

OPENING HOURS

daily from 11:30 to 20:00
(last order 18:00); closed
during New Year

PRICE

1800 yen for a meal;
1100 yen for desserts;
takeaway available

Sincere Garden
シンシア・ガーデン

Housed on the second floor of a small spa, this little cafe serves lots of colourful salads, bright curries and a revolving selection of seasonal sweets. The portions may be a bit small for those with large appetites, but you can fill out your meal with one of their moist muffins or fresh bagels, often available in unusual flavours. Check out their seasonal specials, as you may be able to try vegan versions of Japanese favourites, such as *chirashi zushi*, a 'scattered' sushi dish often served during spring. English menus and a selection of gluten-free options are available.

Top: *You will find light, creative dishes in this cosy second-floor cafe.*

ADDRESS

2-18-5 Jingumae, Shibuya-ku, Tokyo

HOW TO GET THERE

from Harajuku Station's Takeshita Exit, cross the street and enter Takeshita Street. Go straight until you reach the end of the street and find yourself at the pedestrian crossing of the large Meiji Dori street. Cross and take an immediate left onto the little Harajuku Street (look for the half-arch signs). Walk to the end of the street, then take a right, cross the road and continue in the same direction. Eventually you should see a yellow building. Right before the building take a left to find the restaurant.

OPENING HOURS

daily – lunch from 11:00 to 15:00 (last order 14:30); dinner from 17:00 to 22:00 (last order 21:00); Sunday dinner 17:00 to 21:00 (last order 20:00)

PRICE

1300–1600 yen for lunch; budget around 4000 yen for dinner

Mominoki House
モミノキハウス

Chef Yamada has been offering healthy, pesticide-free veggie and brown rice–based meals since 1976, making this restaurant one of the longest-running macrobiotic restaurants in Tokyo. While there are a small number of meat and fish dishes on the menu, it is clear that the majority of diners come looking for vegan lunch sets and seasonal specials. The staples of Japanese macrobiotic cuisine are all present, with subtle seasoning and nicely chewy rice. The regular menu offers crunchy vegan cutlets and thick tofu steaks, but make sure to check out any interesting seasonal dishes, such as noodles or lasagna. English-language menus and English-speaking staff are always on hand and there are a few gluten-free options as well. While a bit pricey, the ease of ordering makes this a safe bet for visiting vegans.

Top: Vegan sushi, a rarity in Japan.

6-13-6 Jingumae,
Shibuya-ku, Tokyo

HOW TO GET THERE

take Exit 4 from Meiji-
Jingumae Station, and
walk straight ahead
crossing the major road.
Turn right and walk until
you reach the second
tiny side street to the left,
right before the Arc'teryx
store. Walk down this
street, then take a
right at the post office.
Keep on going; you will
soon see the shop on
your right.

OPENING HOURS

daily from 10:00 to 20:00

PRICE

380–420 yen for a
doughnut; 600 yen for
the almond milk latte

Good Town Doughnuts
グッドタウンドーナツ

Just off trendy Cat Street, this little joint is Valhalla for
doughnut lovers. Every day they make a handful of
vegan versions of their sweet treats, which are kept in a
separate case next to the non-vegan varieties. It is best
to go early in the day because they do sell out, and
you don't want to miss the perfectly moist doughnuts,
covered with decadent glazes that manage to be
diabetes-inducing but vibrant at the same time. The
Sicilian lemon-poppy doughnut's glaze is fresh and
intense, and their signature smiley mango doughnuts
are sure to put a smile on your face, too. If you want
to add a caffeine rush to your sugar high, they offer
almond milk lattes and American-style coffee with
free refills.

*Top: Look for the retro Little Bakery Tokyo sign. **Bottom right:** Go early to
get the biggest choice of freshly made vegan doughnuts.*

ADDRESS

Sendagaya RF Building,
2-6-3 Sendagaya,
Shibuya-ku, Tokyo

⚓ HOW TO GET THERE

leave via the Main Exit
of Harajuku Station,
then take a right and
follow the large road
until you get to the
Nespresso Cafe. Turn
right and keep going
straight. The shop is just
past the Sendagaya
Elementary School.

🕐 OPENING HOURS

daily from 11:00 to 19:30

¥ PRICE

600–700 yen for a couple
of scoops, a little more if
you select toppings

Kippy's Coco-Cream
キッピーズココクリーム

A Californian import, the creamy coconut-based desserts at Kippy's Coco-Cream are worth the 10-minute walk from the station. All the flavours are made with as few ingredients as possible and no processed sugar, so no flighty sugar highs here! The consistency of the coconut ice cream is very close to dairy-based ice cream, and doesn't have the odd icy texture that's common with soy or rice milk. The cinnamon and coffee date double scoop is a favourite, and the seasonal specials are always something to look forward to. One disclaimer: most of the flavours include raw honey; however, there are always a few that use dates to sweeten the coconut cream instead. It is all written out clearly, so no worries about accidentally buying a honey-based dessert. Kippy's shares the space with a juice and shake shop, in case you want to sneak in some (rather pricey) fruits and veggies.

Bottom: Be sure to check which options are vegan before ordering.

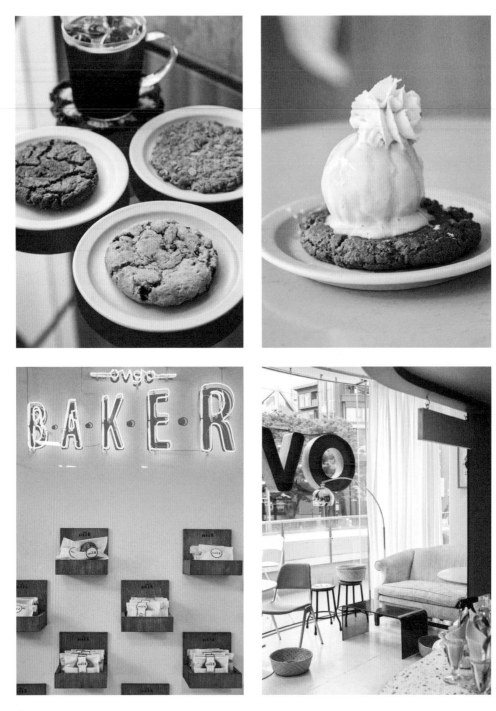

ADDRESS

Laforet Harajuku 2F,
1 -11-6 Jingumae,
Shibuya-ku, Tokyo

HOW TO GET THERE

from Exit 5 of Meiji-
Jingumae Station, take
an immediate left and
you will see the Laforet
department store.

OPENING HOURS

daily from 11:00 to 20:00

PRICE

400–600 yen for baked
goods; around 500 yen
for most drinks; 1980 yen
for the banana split

Ovgo B.A.K.E.R Meiji St.

オブゴベイカー ラフォーレ原宿店

Not only are the decadent desserts at this airy diner-inspired spot vegan, but they also try to reduce their CO_2 footprint by using mainly organic, Japan-grown ingredients. The American-style chewy cookies, delightful 'scookies' (a scone/cookie hybrid) and other daily specials all live up to the shop's motto: 'Doing good tastes so good'. The 'impossible chocolate chip' is one of the best vegan cookies I have ever tasted, but be sure to also sample some of the more Japan-inspired flavours, such as the fragrant matcha coconut, zesty lemon tea and azukinako (flavoured with azuki beans and roasted soy flour).

For die-hard sweet tooths, ramp up your experience by buying one of the ice cream–topped cookie or brownie sundaes … and if you are lucky, you may even be able to order the totally indulgent banana split (but get in early, as they only serve 20 a day!).

*Top: A totally vegan sugar high, thanks to the cookie and ice-cream concoctions available. **Bottom left:** Pick up some cookies to go and enjoy them in nearby Yoyogi Park.*

HOW TO GET THERE
take Exit B1 of
Omotesando Station –
you will see the building
to your left, right after
the major pedestrian
crossing.

OPENING HOURS
daily; vegan course
only available at dinner
from 17:00 to 23:00
(last entry 21:30)

PRICE
3960 yen for the
vegan set

10Zen
薬膳レストラン10ZEN 青山店

During the winter in Japan, hotpot is a major staple
on local dinner tables. However, there are not many
places that offer 100 per cent vegan options. 10Zen
offers a vegan dinner hotpot set with two different
soups, all prepared based on *yakuzen*, traditional
herbal medicine. Dip fresh vegetables, a medley of
Japanese mushrooms, *yuba* (tofu skin) and other
tidbits into the two seasonal soups, and feel your
body warm up from within.

Finish off your dinner like a local by adding the lotus
root udon noodles or mixed rice to the soup at the
end. For those with big appetites, order an extra
plate or two of tofu for an extra protein kick.

Top left: *Try two different types of soup in the same bowl.*
Top right: *Even the desserts are created to promote health.*
Bottom left: *Traditional herbal medicine has never tasted so good.*
Bottom right: *Warm up from the inside out with hotpot.*

Always top on the list of places to visit in Tokyo, the traditional neighbourhood of Asakusa is centred around the hulking red Sensoji Temple. From this point dozens of shopping streets radiate, the major one being Nakamise Dori street which leads straight to the temple from the Kaminarimon Gate, with its distinctive huge red lantern. While this can seem a touristy spot, the smaller covered shopping arcades and back streets are more traditional, a jumble of tea houses, restaurants, interesting little shops and private homes. As you explore, keep your eyes peeled for the 'dangling houses' which are the symbol of Hanayashiki, Japan's oldest amusement park.

Dominating the horizon is the towering Tokyo Skytree which, at 634 metres, is the tallest tower in the world. You can ride up to decks at 350 or 450 metres, for views of the entire city.

Another must-see is Kappabashi, the kitchenware district, a great place to find cute ceramics, plastic food samples and other oddities to bring home. Stretch your explorations out to the Kuramae district, which has a wonderful stationery shop, small-batch chocolate shop and a much more local feel.

Ueno is home to one of the city's largest parks, bustling Ameyoko shopping street and a high concentration of museums including the Tokyo National Museum, National Museum of Nature and Science and Tokyo Metropolitan Art Museum, as well as the beautiful International Library of Children's Literature. Ueno Park is famous for being party central during cherry blossom season, but there is plenty to capture your interest year-round. Be sure to pass by Shinobazu Pond and stroll over to Bentendo Temple, located on a little island in the middle, which is particularly pretty in summer when the lotus flowers are in bloom. The whole park is dotted with pretty temples, shrines, statues and seasonal flower gardens, as well as plenty of spots to stop for coffee or tea.

ASAKUSA/ UENO
浅草・上野

ADDRESS

1-3-3 Hanakawado,
Taito-ku, Tokyo

HOW TO GET THERE

from Asakusa Station's
Exit 5 take a right onto
Edo Dori street, and
then another right at
the first side street.
Walk all the way down
and then turn left. The
restaurant is a couple
of buildings down.

OPENING HOURS

Tuesday–Sunday from
11:30 to 15:00 (closed
Tuesday if Monday is
a public holiday)

PRICE

990–2420 yen

Marugoto Vegan Dining Asakusa

まるごとVeganダイニング浅草

Formerly known as The Farm Cafe, this homely little restaurant is only open for lunch. The fantastic location, just a short walk from Sensoji Temple and right along the riverside park that lines the Sumida River (which has great views of Tokyo Skytree), makes it a popular haven for visiting vegans.

Although they offer two hearty lunch sets (with the B set's offerings of curry, tempura, fried soy meat and veggies being particularly good value), don't miss the *tendon* (tempura rice bowl). Tempura batter usually contains egg, but here you can have a delicious vegan (and even gluten-free, upon request) version of this Japanese classic. If you are a bit tired of rice, the giant focaccia sandwich with grilled soy meat has a subtle kick from the *shio koji* fermented marinade.

*Top: Dig into the generous tempura-topped bowl. **Bottom left:** Or opt for one of their hefty sandwiches, which always hits the spot.*

Shochiku-en
松竹圓カフェ

ADDRESS
2-7-6 Nishiasakusa,
Taito-ku, Tokyo

HOW TO GET THERE
from Exit 1 of
Tawaramachi Station,
walk straight down
the large main road.
When you come to a
pedestrian crossing,
cross to the other side
and keep walking in the
same direction. Keep
going until you see a
building with a giant
chef's head. Without
crossing the road, turn
left onto Kappabashi
Dori street. Take the
fourth side street on the
left, and then another
immediate left.

OPENING HOURS
Friday–Tuesday
from 11:00 to 19:00;
Wednesday–Thursday
from 11:00 to 15:00

PRICE
690–900 yen

This tiny cafe is tucked away just off the main shopping street in Kappabashi. It offers a select range of organic teas, a few burgers for a light meal, and the main reason people visit: the vegan, gluten-free cakes. Among all the options, the rainbow cake reigns supreme. This six-layer, eminently Instagrammable creation gets its signature colours from natural ingredients, such as beetroot (beets), pumpkin (squash) and spinach. As they use natural beet sugar, their cakes have a delicate sweetness enhanced by the fluffy frosting. If you still have room, try the taro cake, a twist on a Taiwanese favourite.

For those who prefer a savoury bite, the 'haru burger' is stuffed with 'egg' made from *yuba* (tofu skin) and vegan cheese, sandwiched between two layers of their homemade cloud-like buns.

Top: Shochiku-en's cakes are too pretty to eat ... almost.
Bottom right: Smoothies and Taiwanese teas are also on the menu.

Sasaya Cafe
ささやカフェ

ADDRESS
1-1-10 Yokokawa,
Sumida-ku, Tokyo

HOW TO GET THERE
the restaurant is a
10-minute walk from
the Tokyo Skytree. From
Exit A1 of Tokyo Skytree
Station (or from the plaza
in front of the entrance
to Skytree), turn left and
cross the bridge over
the small river. Cross the
street at the intersection,
and stick to the right side
of the road going straight
ahead. Around halfway
you will pass the Salt
and Tobacco Museum
(on your right). Cross
the large intersection
with Kasuga Dori street.
Ahead of you and a bit to
the right you should see
some bamboo and the
Sasaya Cafe sign, which
has an image of Mt. Fuji.

OPENING HOURS
daily (with occasional
days off) from 08:30
to 18:00

PRICE
800–1400 yen for a
meal; around 500 yen
for baked goods

Housed in a renovated factory overlooking a section of the long, skinny Oyokogawa Shinsui park which runs between the Skytree and Kinshicho Station, Sasaya is surprisingly large and airy, a welcome addition in a city where niche restaurants tend towards the cramped. The menu is small, but happily also written in English. There is usually at least one gluten-free option available which is less obvious, but the staff are happy to help.

The Indian-style meals, made with organic, domestically grown ingredients, are comforting, but the real standout is the fried tempeh cutlet, which is nicely crunchy on the outside and thick with fat soybeans. Sasaya has a rotating selection of sandwiches and monthly Asian-inspired specials. If you are there bright and early, you may be rewarded by tofu cheese toast, vegan quiche or freshly baked muffins, all of which pair nicely with the sweet, spicy masala chai.

Top: The Indian-inspired sets at Sasaya Cafe, which is just a short walk from Skytree. *Bottom left:* Chill out with a matcha latte or some chai.

1-2-11 Ryusen, Taito-ku, Tokyo

🛥 **HOW TO GET THERE**

from Iriya Station take Exit 3, and go straight ahead until you reach a pedestrian crossing. Cross and take an immediate right. Continue on until you are almost at the end of the street, and take the last side street on the left (look for the white sign with the character 梵 on it) before reaching the wide road ahead. The restaurant is located in the second building on your left.

🕐 **OPENING HOURS**

Thursday–Tuesday lunch from 12:00 to 15:00 (last order 13:00); dinner from 17:30 to 21:00 (last order 19:00) on weekdays and from 17:00 to 20:00 (last order 18:00) on weekends. Reservations are highly recommended (03-3872-0375; basic English spoken).

¥ **PRICE**

weekday lunch around 3450 or 5000 yen; dinner courses available for 6000, 8000 or 10,000 yen.

Fucha Bon
普茶料理 梵

The private *tatami* rooms, serene decor and refreshingly unpretentious, friendly service at Bon blow you away even before you have a chance to taste their *fucha* cuisine, a Chinese version of Japanese *shojin ryori* Buddhist meals. The restaurant has been around since 1972, originally aimed at serving Zen-influenced dishes at temple functions, and it is clear that it is still a popular spot for families to come together after attending various Buddhist rites.

The procession of delicate, intricate dishes begins with a light tea and *rakugan* pressed-sugar sweet, and then takes off into a folly of seasonal tastes, with a fried *asagao* flower and faux abalone with lemon being just two highlights from a recent visit. A few staples of *fucha* are present in every meal, such as *unpen*, a ginger-laced, thickened soup made with leftover veggies, which goes along with the waste-not philosophy of this cuisine. Other showstoppers are the intense sesame tofu and their famous fried eggplant covered in a hearty miso sauce. Light eaters and those on a budget should opt for the weekday lunch courses, as the more expensive courses are extremely filling. Make sure to wear matching, clean, hole-free socks, as you will be expected to remove your shoes before entering the *tatami* room.

Top: The intricate dishes at Fucha Bon will have you reaching for your camera.

ADDRESS
1-1-2 Ryusen, Taito-ku, Tokyo

HOW TO GET THERE
follow the directions for reaching Fucha Bon on page 76; the restaurant is just a couple of doors up.

OPENING HOURS
Monday, Thursday and Friday from 11:00 to 20:00 (last order 19:30); Saturday and Sunday from 10:00 to 17:00 (last order 16:30)

PRICE
1250–2000 yen; sweets 300–500 yen

PQ's
ピーキューズ

This cosy, LGBTQ+-friendly restaurant is located near Otori Shrine, known for its colourful Tori no Ichi festival and market in November, and is close to Yoshiwara, the former red-light district that flourished in the Edo period.

If your budget doesn't stretch far enough for nearby Fucha Bon, the incredibly beautiful curries at PQ's are a more affordable delight. Ranging from pink to blue, purple and yellow (depending on the spices and ingredients available), and with the rice formed into a crescent-moon shape and carefully selected toppings, these curries will be among the prettiest you have ever seen (and the flavours are equally satisfying and complex). For a teatime break, the black sesame latte and one of the freshly baked muffins make a lovely treat to enjoy by the large windows.

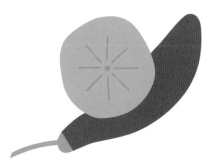

Top: Brightly coloured curries are just one of the delights at PQ's.

ADDRESS
Ecute Ueno 3F, 7-1-1
Ueno, Taito ku, Tokyo

HOW TO GET THERE
the shop is located
inside Ueno Station's
gates, so you will need
to buy a ticket if you are
not already inside. The
restaurant is easiest to
reach from the Park or
Iriya exits, and is across
from Platform 8. Look
for maps of the Ecute
restaurant locations
inside the station.

OPENING HOURS
Monday–Friday
from 10:00 to 22:00;
Saturday–Sunday
from 10:00 to 21:00
(last order 30 minutes
before closing)

PRICE
850–1500 yen for a meal;
side dishes from 250 yen

T's Tantan Ecute Ueno
T'sたんたん エキュート上野店

Ecute ueno is the second branch of the beloved T's
Tantan vegan ramen shop located in Tokyo Station.
It offers all of their signature *tantan* ramen bowls,
along with a small selection of side dishes, such as
their justly famous *gyoza* dumplings and mini rice bowl
topped with vegan *chashu* (braised pork). The golden
sesame *tanmen* has a creamy soup with a kick of
chilli, and the soupless *tantan* is a good lighter option,
especially topped with an extra serving of coriander.
They also have a branch in Ikebukuro Station.

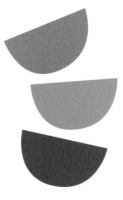

Top: A bowl of rich tantan *ramen is sure to put a smile on your face.*
*Bottom: This ramen shop inside Ueno Station has a variety of noodle
dishes to choose from.*

Roppongi is one of Tokyo's party areas, particularly for the expat community, and the main drawcards during the day are the many art galleries, such as the Mori Art Museum, located at the very top of the vertiginous Mori Tower, as well as the Suntory Museum of Art and National Art Center. Visitors can also enjoy shopping opportunities and pleasant gardens near Tokyo Midtown. The Aoyama Cemetery is a nice spot for a quiet stroll, and a must-see during cherry blossom season when the tombs are lightened by fluffy *sakura* blossoms. Around November to Christmas, the Keyakizaka hill hosts wonderful winter illuminations.

This is also where you will find Gonpachi, the famous restaurant featured in the Tarantino movie *Kill Bill*. For those who want to experience the atmosphere of this visually dramatic spot, they do offer a vegan *nigiri* sushi set and a few grilled veggie skewers.

ROPPONGI

六本木

ADDRESS

5-1-10 Roppongi,
Minato-ku, Tokyo

HOW TO GET THERE

turn right out of
Roppongi Station's
4a Exit, then immediately
take another right onto
Imoaraizaka Street
and walk for about
100 metres (330 feet)

OPENING HOURS

daily – Falafel Brothers
from 11:00 to 21:00;
The Brothers Corner
from 08:30 to 20:00

PRICE

1000–1450 yen for
lunch; budget 2000 yen
for dinner

Falafel Brothers &
The Brothers Corner

ファラフェルブラザーズ & ザ ブラザーズ コーナー

Tokyo's first falafel chain (now with three branches, including one in Shibuya and Ebisu), Falafel Brothers arrived in 2017 and immediately made waves among expats who were craving giant pita sandwiches stuffed with the ever-popular vegan staple.

In Roppongi they have taken over a corner with two adjacent shops. The original Falafel Brothers outpost is a small but amusingly quirky spot that serves generously portioned falafel-filled pitas, hummus plates and colourful salad bowls, along with a selection of vegan desserts. If you have never tried *renkon* (lotus root), try the fried version they offer as a side dish for the set menus.

If you are looking for something less chickpea-focused, the newer Brothers Corner offers pressed sandwiches filled with ingredients like vegan ham, vegan egg or veggies, along with wraps. The pizza slices are also good for a quick meal on the go, or linger longer over the indulgent pecan pie and 'crookie', a warmed cookie topped with ice cream.

Top: In addition to falafel, generous bowls of hummus and fresh sandwiches are also available.

🗺 HOW TO GET THERE

turn your back to The
Brother's Corner (see
page 85) and walk
straight down the road
directly in front of you.
On the right you will
see a black, mirrored
building; the restaurant
is on the 3rd floor.

⏰ OPENING HOURS

Monday–Saturday lunch
from 11:30 to 15:00 (last
order 14:00); dinner
from 17:30 to 23:00 (last
order 21:30). Closed
on public holidays.
Reservations essential.

¥ PRICE

8800 yen for the
lunch course; 12,100–
14,300 yen for dinner

Sougo
宗胡

Michelin-star chef Daisuke Nomura has *shojin ryori*
Buddhist cuisine in his blood, and for many years
was the executive chef of his family restaurant, the
illustrious Daigo near Tokyo Tower. At Sougo he is
seeking to make this traditional form of cuisine a
little more relaxed and accessible, and offers fully
vegan courses (as regular *shojin ryori* can sometimes
contain some fish broth or egg). From seats at the
sleek, modern counter, you can watch the chefs do
their magic.

In typical Japanese style, the menu changes every
three weeks to capture the flavours of every small
change in season. If you are lucky you may get to
try some 'sushi', with vegetables expertly used to
re-create eel or salmon. The desserts, which often
in traditional Japanese cuisine can be a bit boring,
are innovative and surprising. Be sure to book a
table in advance.

*Top: Elegant Japanese cuisine at its finest. **Bottom:** The open kitchen
allows you to watch the chefs create the detailed plates.*

ADDRESS
2F, 3-1-19 Nishi Azabu, Minato-ku, Tokyo

⚒ HOW TO GET THERE
from Exit 1A of Roppongi Station, walk straight ahead for about 150 metres (450 feet). The restaurant will be on your left, on the 2nd floor.

🕐 OPENING HOURS
daily – lunch from 11:30 to 14:00; dinner from 17:00 to 21:00. Closed for lunch on public holidays.

ⓨ PRICE
around 2400 yen for a large pizza

Pizzakaya
ピザカヤ

Getting a bit tired of Japanese food? Need a hit of something wonderfully cheesy and carb-filled? Then head to the fire engine–red embrace of this friendly joint that offers regular, vegan and gluten-free pizzas.

The cashew cheese they use to top their vegan pizzas is creamy and rich, and matches particularly well with the 'wild wild mushroom', a medley of tasty Japanese mushrooms such as maitake and shiitake. For something a bit different, the 'yupanqui pie' has stripes of organic white, black, green and pink pepper from Ecuador.

The portions are quite hefty, so ordering one large pizza, along with a couple of veggie appetisers and a pint from their line-up of 10 different craft beers should be plenty for two people. Just be aware that in Japan pizza tends to be much more expensive than other countries, so don't be shocked at the price.

Top: The hearty vegan pizzas can make a nice break from rice.

ADDRESS

5-10-32 Roppongi,
Minato-ku, Tokyo

⚐ HOW TO GET THERE

turn right out of Exit 3
of Roppongi Station,
then turn right again
into a small sloping
street right after the
Almond Cafe. Follow
the street downwards,
passing Falafel Brothers.
Eventually you should
see the Step Roppongi
building on your right.
Continue straight until
you see a brown-and-
white-striped building
on your left. The shop
is in the next building –
look for the sign and
wheatgrass plants in
the windows.

🕒 OPENING HOURS

Monday–Saturday lunch
from 11:00 to 15:00;
dinner from 17:30 to
20:00; Sunday lunch
from 11:00 to 14:00. Last
order is 30 minutes
before closing.

Ⓨ PRICE

1000–1700 yen for the
vegan buffet, kefir soy-
milk smoothies from
700 yen

.RAW
ドットロー

If you are feeling a bit rundown and missing fresh
veggies, .RAW offers the best-priced salad bar in town.
Choose from around 40 different organic veggies and
grains, with lots of homemade salad dressings (the
bright-red beetroot dressing is particularly nice) and
extra-affordable side dishes, such as bread, soup and
vegan deli items to bulk things up if needed. They
also have some non-vegan options available. Their
kefir soy-milk smoothies, especially the blueberry-
flavoured ones, are great for a late breakfast or as
a pick-me-up on a hot day.

*Top and bottom right: Choose from a wide variety of ingredients to build
your own salad. Bottom left: Grab a smoothie for an on-the-go snack.*

Shimokitazawa is often compared to Brooklyn... at least by locals! A warren of twisty streets with tons of vintage clothing stores, record shops, live houses (live music venues), bookshops, galleries and dozens of coffee joints, 'Shimo' is a cheerful mishmash that attracts lots of young, artistic folk. There are often open-air markets, with creators selling all sorts of interesting handmade items.

As with many parts of Tokyo, some of the best places in Shimo are tucked away in the side streets, and it can be a bit difficult to navigate, exacerbated by the expansion work done on its station. The warren of bars, which was once a main feature of the area, has been stripped down to only a few remaining spots, in order to make room for the new station buildings, which is a pity. Nonetheless, it is a great place to wander about while sipping a cup of coffee. Ex Libris is a particular favourite for coffee connoisseurs. Keep an eye out for the colourful shutter art, too!

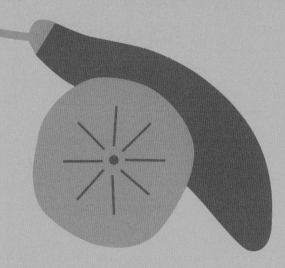

SHIMOKITAZAWA

下北沢

🏔 **HOW TO GET THERE**

take West Exit 1 of Shimokitazawa Station and take an immediate right (away from the train tracks). Keep going straight on this road for about 5 minutes; eventually you will pass the large white Seitoku school building on your left. Keep walking until you reach a small intersection, then take a left-right before a tiny park/sitting area. You will eventually pass another school, and the shop will be a little past this, on your right. It is a very unassuming place, so keep an eye out.

🕐 **OPENING HOURS**

Tuesday–Sunday from 17:00 to 23:00

¥ **PRICE**

950–1400 yen for curries and ramen; 600 yen for side dishes

Chabuzen
薬膳食堂ちゃぶ膳

This may well be not only one of the smallest vegan restaurants in Tokyo, but also one of the most overlooked. The owner is very open to visitors from abroad, and is a big fan of brown rice yeast and *yakuzen* (traditional herbal medicine). But don't think that the hippy-ness of the ingredients has any negative effect on the food, which is all quite tasty, Asian-vegan friendly and a bit offbeat. The little fresh salads are one of the highlights, veering towards Indonesian flavours with lots of interesting herbs mixed in.

The ramen bowls are light and topped with more herbs, and the curries are surprisingly complex, even when they contain no garlic or onion. Can't decide? The Nirvana curry ramen will satisfy both cravings. Another star is the rare vegan *oden*, a winter favourite with various ingredients simmered whole in stock. On chilly days, warm up with the white curry, which resembles a hearty dish known as 'cream stew', a bechamel-based household favourite in Japan.

Top left: The inventive ramen includes traditional medicinal herbs.
Top right: Try the freshly fried gyoza served with a punchy sauce.

Superiority Burger

スペリオリティー バーガー

An outpost of the legendary punk/vegan burger spot in New York's East Village, Superiority Burger in Tokyo serves the same standard gloriously junky and messy sandwiches, joined by a few new creations with a distinctly Japanese twist.

The TFT (Tokyo Fried Tofu) burger will fill the void in your life you didn't even know you had ... like KFC, but without the cruelty. The intensely crispy tofu gets a kick from being marinated in pickle juice and is topped with a creamy slaw (and accompanied by delicious fried potatoes). Another absolute must-try is the New Japan Creation, a bun stuffed with seasoned *yuba* (tofu skin), with a sesame sauce, punchy herbs and a surprising hint of mint. While you are at it, try the burnt broccoli salad, which comes with an intense, savoury eggplant dip. Superiority Burger only has three tiny tables, so visiting at slightly off-peak times is best.

*Top left: The TFT burger is an over-the-top crunchy delight. **Bottom right**: Make sure you leave room for one of their excellent ice creams.*

Reload 2F, 3-19-20 Kitazawa, Setagaya-ku, Tokyo

HOW TO GET THERE

the bakery is halfway between Shimokitazawa and Higashi-kitazawa stations. Using a map app is your best bet here, as there is still construction going on. It's about a 4-minute walk from the East Exit of Shimokitazawa Station.

OPENING HOURS

Wednesday–Sunday from 08:30 to 18:00; Tuesday from 10:00 to 18:00. Closed Mondays.

PRICE

300–500 yen

Universal Bakes Nicome
ユニバーサルベイクス ニコメ

Doughnuts, muffins and croissants, oh my! This pint-sized bakery is on the second floor of the trendy Reload complex, and has terrace seats where you can enjoy the top-notch vegan pastries. Plant-based expats flock here to quench their croissant cravings, but the shop also offers a variety of interesting creations, such as single slices of French toast topped with seasonal fruit, fluffy *coppe pan* rolls stuffed with butter and red bean paste, and fragrant cinnamon rolls. They also serve basic coffee drinks, making this a great spot for a sweet breakfast on a sunny day.

The main branch of Universal Bakes is about a 10-minute walk away, tucked away in a quiet residential area right behind neighbouring Setagaya-Daita Station. They have a number of more savoury options and traditional breads, ideal for breakfast the next morning.

Top: You'll find savoury and sweet bakes galore at Universal Bakes.
Bottom left: The decorated doughnuts are always worth sampling.
Bottom right: Start your morning off right with an iced latte and a selection of sweet treats.

AIRPORTS & TOKYO STATION
空港 & 東京駅

Until just a few years ago most of Tokyo's major transport hubs were disappointing deserts for plant-based foodies. However, there have been some positive changes, mainly thanks to the T's Tantan ramen chain stepping in to fill the gap.

NARITA AIRPORT

成田空港

Despite being known as Tokyo's main international airport, this massive hub is actually located quite far away from the city itself, in neighbouring Chiba Prefecture (which is also home to Tokyo Disneyland). Be prepared for a long train ride on the pricey Narita Express to get into central Tokyo.

T's Tantan

T'sたんたん

Get your first or last Tokyo ramen fix at the iconic vegan noodle shop. Turn to the Tokyo Station section on page 102 for information on the menu.

◉ **ADDRESS:** Terminal 2, 4th floor, outside the boarding gates

HANEDA AIRPORT

羽田空港

If you can wing it, arriving and departing from Haneda Airport is the way to go. It is far closer to central Tokyo, more walkable and has much more to see and do. In addition to the cafe below, GGG (before the gates) and Chaya Cafe Organic Coffee & Bread (inside the gates) also offer a few vegan options.

HealthyTOKYO Cafe & Shop

HealthyTOKYO 羽田空港店

It's worth arriving early for check-in to try the 100 per cent vegan menu from Japan's CBD pioneer. The gluten-free lasagna is hefty and rich, or buy the caprese sandwich and a couple of muffins to go if you want to avoid mediocre airline food. The CBD chocolates might be just the thing for nervous fliers.

◉ **ADDRESS:** Terminal 2, 3rd floor, outside the boarding gates

TOKYO STATION
東京駅

Tokyo Station is the main hub for *shinkansen* (bullet trains) and a grand intersection for train lines from all ends of the city. This huge station is also quite close to the Nihonbashi and Ginza areas. The original section of the station, which dates back to the early 1900s, is a lovely piece of Meiji architecture worth a look. Nearby you will find the Imperial Palace and the large Imperial East Gardens, which are open to the public.

Within the station, it is easy to get lost among the hundreds of shops, exits, restaurants and 'salarymen' rushing to and fro. However, it is worth braving the labyrinth, as Tokyo Station is home to two excellent vegan ramen joints!

T's Tantan
T'sたんたん

Follow the signs for the red Keiyo Line to reach one of the first, and best, vegan ramen joints in town. Their specialty is obviously *tantan* (ground meat) ramen, of which they offer different varieties, all fragrant with sesame oil and with enough oomph to win over carnivores. The black sesame ramen is the perfect dish to dig into on a chilly day. Make sure you also order the *gyoza*.

⊙ **ADDRESS:** Keiyo Street inside Tokyo Station gates, near the bullet train gates

Sora no Iro NIPPON
ソラノイロNIPPON

This shop is located in Ramen Street in the basement floor of Tokyo Station's First Avenue shopping area. It is easily accessible from the Yaesu side of the station.

Earning a mention in the Michelin Guide, Sora no Iro's version of ramen is both inventive and colourful. Instead of recreating flavours common to meat-based soups, they draw out the full depth of flavour from vegetables, creating a hearty, creamy base for the noodles, which are then garnished with seasonal veggies.

⊙ **ADDRESS:** Ramen Street in First Avenue, Tokyo Station

Tokyo Station is home to some truly awesome vegan ramen spots.

穴場スポット

OFF THE BEATEN PATH

   If you are looking to see a more local side of Tokyo, there are a number of neighbourhoods just off the beaten track that offer top-notch food and a few interesting sights.
   The Toyoko Line, Hibiya Line and Chuo Line seem to be popular areas for plant-based cafes and restaurants to congregate, making it possible to hop from one to the other while exploring. In each of the following sections you will also find a bit of information about nearby sights and more famous spots on the same train line, so you can plan your outings with ease.

Within walking distance of Shibuya, Daikanyama, Hiroo and Nakameguro, Ebisu is easy to get to and known as one of the top well-heeled neighbourhoods of Tokyo. Named after the Ebisu brewery, which used to be located here, the area is home to the Museum of Yebisu Beer where you can try some samples for less than 500 yen. Take a quick stroll around the Ebisu Garden Place area to check out the incongruous Joel Robuchon restaurant, which looks like a small castle. During the Christmas season, the area becomes a hot date spot, with lots of couples coming to see a giant Baccarat crystal chandelier lit up after dark.

Art lovers will like the neighbourhood for its multitude of small galleries, the Tokyo Metropolitan Museum of Photography, the bijou Yamatane Museum of Art's Japanese paintings and the eclectic Matsuoka Museum of Art.

Ebisu is accessible from Ebisu Station, which is one stop away from Shibuya on the JR Yamanote Line. If you are travelling with the JR Pass, this train line will be your major artery around the city.

Daikanyama is dotted with designer shops, interior-design stores, interesting cafes and lots of very expensive housing. Sightseeing-wise, the Kyu Asakura house, built in 1919, is a wonderful example of combined Japanese and Western architecture, with a pleasant garden with spots to sit and gaze at it contemplatively. At Daikanyama T-Site you can explore the huge, artsy Tsutaya bookshop, which has a decent selection of English-language books, as well as a constantly changing range of crafts, foods, art and other intriguing things for sale. Beer lovers will want to check out the gorgeous Spring Valley Brewery, which has seasonal craft beers and is housed in a wood and glass structure that feels like it could just take flight.

Daikanyama is on the Toyoko Line, just one stop from Shibuya.

EBISU/ DAIKANYAMA

恵比寿・代官山

🚶 **HOW TO GET THERE**

standing with your back
to the ticket gates of
the West Exit of Ebisu
Station, take a right (you
should see a Montbell
store), then take a left
onto the small road.
Once you reach the
large Komazawa Dori
street take a right again,
and cross at the first
pedestrian crossing on
your left. Right in front
of you there will be a
smaller road between
two large buildings (one
is white with a vertical
strip of windows). Go
straight, and you will find
the cafe on the left side;
look for the green sign.

🕐 **OPENING HOURS**

Thursday–Tuesday
from 11:00 to 20:00
(last order 19:30)

¥ **PRICE**

1000–1500 yen for lunch;
budget 2000–3000 yen
for dinner; pancakes
around 1100 yen

KO-SO CAFE
コウソカフェ ビオライズ

Literally translated as 'enzyme cafe', this colourful
little restaurant sneaks brown rice and a fermented
'enzyme paste' made with 88 different veggies into
most of its dishes. Although it sounds a bit odd, it may
well be the secret to the complex flavours the chefs
whip up with aplomb. The cafe is mainly famous for
its colourful vegan pancakes, in particular the cocoa-
scented 'detox pancakes', but the large selection
of seasonal dishes should not be underestimated.
The vegan pizza's brown rice crust serves as a base
for a well-balanced combination of punchy tomato
sauce and creamy 'cheese'. Be aware that the pasta
sauces are Japanese-style, so they tend to be soupier
than one would expect from Italian cuisine. KO-SO is
certified halal and vegan, and has quite a few gluten-
free options on their menu, including 100 per cent
buckwheat pancakes.

Top: Healthy cakes and pancakes are just some of the draws at KO-SO.
Bottom right: Get a boost of greens (and enzymes) in your daily bowl.

ADDRESS

8F, 3-17-14 Higashi, Shibuya-ku, Tokyo, Japan

HOW TO GET THERE

follow the instructions to get to KO-SO cafe on page 108. Once you pass it, turn right before the 'cracked' building. Go to the end of the little street and the building will be right in front of you; the restaurant is on the 8th floor.

OPENING HOURS

Wednesday–Monday lunch from 11:30 to 15:00; dinner from 18:00 to 22:00

PRICE

1480–1880 yen for lunch; budget 3000–4000 yen for dinner. Course meals available by reservation.

Hemp Cafe
ヘンプカフェトーキョー

Hemp Cafe has a wide, mainly (but not only) Mexican-influenced selection of vegan and hemp-based dishes to try. For lunch get the *bibimbap*, a Korean rice bowl with vegan meat, homemade kimchi and other toppings served in a sizzling hot stone bowl. At dinnertime, your best bet is to order a few dishes to share, such as the rather good Korean-style 'meat' sushi, along with some stone-grilled nachos or tacos, and treat yourself to a couple of the interesting cocktails, such as the homemade ginger or apple cinnamon mojitos.

All their drinks can be laced with a shot of CBD for an additional 300 yen, and the entire dessert menu (which features a decadent brownie ice-cream sandwich) already contains CBD, so you are sure to leave feeling full and mellow.

Top: A sizzling plate of spicy *bibimbap*. ***Bottom right:*** *Wash down your tacos with some CBD beer.*

HOW TO GET THERE

from the east exit of
Ebisu Station, follow the
road to the right and
walk down the hill until
you reach a crossroads.
Keeping towards the left,
cross the road and take
the smaller road that
curves towards the left.
It is in the third building
on the 2nd floor.

OPENING HOURS

daily – lunch from 11:30
to 15:00 (last order 14:30);
dinner from 17:00 to
23:00 (last order 22:00).
Monday lunch only.

PRICE

1100 yen for lunch;
around 3000 yen and up
for dinner, more if you
order wine

SUMI-BIO
スミビオ

With a polished wooden bar counter, chandeliers
and chandeliers and private little tables, this organic restaurant is a
great place for a special occasion, or to take friends
and family who are not vegan, as they also serve
meat dishes.

Lunch is one of the best deals in the Ebisu area, with
a selection of sets featuring Chinese dishes such as
spicy *mapo tofu* and *hoikoro* (a miso-based stir-fry).
Dinner is more varied, and their seasonal specials
focus around organic veggies they buy directly from
nearby farmers. In winter opt for the *nabe* hotpot, with
a creamy soy milk–based soup and lots of interesting
mushrooms. For dessert, don't miss the melt-in-your-
mouth *nama* chocolates. The staff don't speak English,
but are familiar with veganism, so can point out which
dishes are safe.

*SUMI-BIO is one of the best budget-friendly spots for lunch in
classy Ebisu.*

🥾 **HOW TO GET THERE**
from the North Exit of
Daikanyama Station,
cross the overpass
towards the little park,
then go down the stairs
and turn right (the park
should be on your left).
Follow the road and walk
through the intersection,
then take the second
right and go up the stairs.

🕐 **OPENING HOURS**
Tuesday–Sunday from
12:00 to 18:00

¥ **PRICE**
1300–1900 yen

Hatena

はてな代官山

Vegan. Doughnut. Burgers. Need one say more? Grab one of the terrace seats at this quirky eatery and give yourself over to the pleasures of cruelty-free junk food. The *tatsuta* (double-fried 'chicken') and *teriyaki* burgers have heaps of juicy soy meat, sandwiched between fluffy, unglazed doughnut buns. If that sounds a bit much, the 'chef's choice' focaccia is cooked in a small cast-iron pan that gives a perfect crisp base and is smothered in a mosaic of colourful, seasonal organic veggies.

If you prefer to stop by for an afternoon snack (or are hankering for dessert), get the raspberry, cream and chocolate bar–filled doughnut, along with an iced soy latte (that comes with surprise ice cubes). They also only use metal straws, which is a nice bonus.

Top: The pinnacle of vegan junk food: the doughnut burger! **Bottom left:** *The burger is not to be outdone by the sweet doughnut sandwich!*

A little out of central Tokyo, Jiyugaoka is considered a chic spot to live, and is thus filled with small boutiques, fancy cafes and elegant houses. While it's not a major centre for sightseeing, in spring the cherry blossoms are in full bloom on the main shopping street. Not far from the station, the La Vita complex re-creates a tiny bit of Venice (complete with canals and even a gondola). Right across the street you will find Kosouan, a lovely teahouse which was once the home of the daughter of Natsume Soseki, one of Japan's most famous writers. There are lots of little streets to explore and a few unobtrusive shrines and temples.

Another offbeat location to check out is the Jiyugaoka Department Store which, despite the name, resembles more of a retro indoor bazaar. The entrance is right by the station's Central Exit. Look to the right – it is the unassuming entrance with kitchenware stacked nearby. The long, narrow corridors are lined with all sorts of oddities. Kimono shops adjoin pickled veggie stores and shops selling antique jewellery, household ceramics, beauty products and anything else you can think of, making for an eclectic atmosphere. The basement is equally intriguing.

Jiyugaoka Station is on the Toyoko Line, making it an easy side trip from Shibuya and Nakameguro, or a good place to stop on the way to or from Yokohama (see pages 144–147).

JIYUGAOKA

自由が丘

T's Restaurant

T's レストラン

ADDRESS

Luz Jiyugaoka Building,
2-2-9-6 Jiyugaoka,
Meguro-ku, Tokyo

HOW TO GET THERE

from the Central Exit
of Jiyugaoka Station,
take the third street on
your right. Keep going
straight, and look for
the Luz building on your
left. The restaurant is in
the basement.

OPENING HOURS

daily from 11:00 to 21:00
(last order 20:30)

PRICE

1350–1500 yen for lunch;
around 2500–3000 yen
for dinner; teatime cakes
around 600–700 yen

A personal favourite, a meal at T's is always a pleasure. The sheer luxury of choice and the presence of comfort food such as lasagna and *doria* (a creamy rice gratin) on the menu are two reasons why this restaurant has such an important place in the heart of most Tokyo vegans. While everything they whip up in the open kitchen is great, there are a few standout dishes. The *yurinchi karaage* (fried 'chicken' tossed in a savoury, vinegary Chinese sauce) or garlicky 'shrimp' *ahijo* is the perfect prelude to the creamy, bubbly lasagna or their incredible *tantanmen* spicy ramen with minced 'meat', one of their signature dishes. For dessert, the chocolate ganache cake or matcha parfait are indulgent, without being cloying or overly sweet.

The only thing that mars the excellence of this spot is the coffee, which is bland. Opt for one of the berry or herb cordials instead, which are particularly nice during the hot summer months. Find out about their ramen shop in Tokyo Station on page 102.

Top: The grilled curry is topped with bubbling melted 'cheese'.
Bottom left: Don't miss the doria, a favourite local comfort food.

Saido
菜道

ADDRESS
2-15-10 Jiyugaoka,
Meguro-ku, Tokyo

HOW TO GET THERE
from the Central Exit
of Jiyugaoka Station,
take a left following the
roundabout. Take the
street to the left, and
follow it as it curves
into Hilo Street (do not
cross the railway tracks).
Walk straight through
the intersection, then
take the first right. The
restaurant is three
buildings down; look
for the plants.

OPENING HOURS
Tuesday–Thursday
lunch from 12:00 to
15:00; dinner from 18:00
to 20:00. Reservations
recommended.

PRICE
2000–3000 yen for
lunch; cafe items around
800–1200 yen; 3000–
10,000 yen for dinner

Saido was voted the world's best vegan restaurant by HappyCow in 2019, which is high praise indeed. The hype is deserved, but it does mean that making a reservation is a good idea. The vibe is unpretentious and friendly, ideal if you want to sample some truly world-class vegan eats but want to skip the stiff service and white tablecloths.

The food is beautifully presented, and captures some of the flavours usually only associated with Japanese meat dishes. The *unagi* ('eel') is a delight, capturing the pillowy texture and the sweet and savoury combination of the *kabayaki* sauce. You can also sample vegan *yakitori* ('chicken' skewers), colourful ramen topped with an astounding vegan egg, and *katsudon*, a Japanese lunchtime favourite of a fried cutlet on a bed of rice. For the full experience, opt for one of the course meals, which includes creative dishes such as a smoke-wreathed salad and blueberry cheesecake that looks like a bonsai tree!

Top: The course menus allow you to try a variety of Saido's creative dishes. ***Bottom left:*** You never know what cool concept the chef will cook up!

121

Strung along the Meguro River, this classy neighbourhood is a favourite spot of Japanese celebrities, wealthy expats and ladies who lunch with small fluffy dogs in tow. The entire river, which extends all the way to Gotanda and Osaki, is lined with huge, old cherry trees, making it a very popular place to visit in spring. In winter the same trees are decked out with fairy lights, for a romantic evening stroll, and in the summer the tree cover makes it cooler than the rest of the sweltering city. Off the main drag there are a few cute *shoutengai* (traditional shopping streets) and the small Sato Sakura Museum of Art, dedicated to various depictions of cherry blossoms.

Nakameguro Station is on both the Hibiya and Toyoko lines, and is just two stops away from Shibuya.

NAKAMEGURO

中目黒

5-2-7 Higashiyama,
Moguro ku, Tokyo

HOW TO GET THERE

from Nakameguro
Station's East Exit,
turn left onto the large
Yamate Dori street.
Walk straight for about
10 minutes, until you see
the Starbucks Reserve
Roastery building on your
right. Keep going straight
through the intersection,
then take the first left
and walk down for
100 metres (330 feet).

OPENING HOURS

daily from 9:00 to 18:00

PRICE

around 1500–1700 yen
for a meal; 310–600 yen
for baked goods

Alaska Zwei
アラスカ ツヴァイ

Don't be fooled by the name – this shabby-chic cafe has absolutely nothing to do with Alaska. The menu is small but carefully thought out, with brown rice, curry, soup and salad plates that change daily. The brown rice plate is a good choice if you want to try a little bit of everything, and usually centres around a main of *karaage* or another soy-meat option in a savoury sauce, surrounded by a number of deli sides. Portions are generous and always bursting with colour.

The vegan *banh mi* and tofu *katsu* cutlet sandwiches are made with olive oil–rich focaccia bread, and their range of desserts – particularly the muffins – are another highlight (and available to take away). On a chilly day be sure to order the mint hot chocolate.

*Bottom left: The daily rice plate is always a good choice. **Bottom right:** Alaska Zwei has a great selection of baked goods and snacks you can buy to go.*

125

🛶 HOW TO GET THERE
it is about a 10-minute
walk from Nakameguro
Station, but easy to find.
Exit the Main Exit of
Nakameguro Station, and
turn right. Pass a large
building with modern art
statues, and take a right
onto a shopping street.
Keep walking down the
shopping street, then
take the third right. Then
turn right again following
the train track overhead.

🕐 OPENING HOURS
weekdays from 18:00
to 4:00 (closed on
Tuesdays); weekends
from 12:00 to 4:00

¥ PRICE
850–1500 yen,
depending on toppings
and sides

Shin-Shin Sausage Club
シンシン ソーセージ倶楽部

This is one for the true night owls, as this pocket-sized,
bright-pink hot-dog joint is open until 4 am in the
morning! They offer both chicken and vegan sausages
that you can customise with an array of toppings. If
you can't decide, choose the 'original' topped with
vegan meat sauce for the full American-style chilli dog
experience, and remind yourself of where you are with
one of the thickshakes in popular Japanese flavours
such as matcha, black sesame or *hojicha* (roasted tea).
If you want something a bit stronger, they offer a variety
of affordable highball cocktails.

*Top: Pop by Shin-Shin after a night on the town and create your
perfect hot dog.*

ADDRESS

2-9-36 Kamimeguro,
Meguro-ku, Tokyo

HOW TO GET THERE

from the South Exit of
Nakameguro Station
take a left, then follow
the small road you will
see to the left. You
should see the gelateria
straight ahead.

OPENING HOURS

Friday–Wednesday from
12:00 to 20:00

PRICE

600–700 yen for gelato

Premarché Gelateria
プレマルシェ・ジェラテリア

Make sure you leave room for dessert when eating in Nakameguro, because you will definitely want to stop by this award-winning gelateria. Just pay attention when making your selection, as the gelati are divided into milk-based and vegan options (which are clearly marked). There are so many flavours to choose from that it will take you a while to settle on two. Selections change depending on the season, but a few standouts are the 'Kyoto white miso', which tastes like a rich cheesecake with a kick of umami at the end, the charcoal-blended 'ninja' and, if you are lucky, the *shiso* perilla-flavoured sorbet.

Top: So many flavours, so little time ...

HOW TO GET THERE

it is about a 10-minute walk from Nakameguro Station, but easy to find. Exit the Main Gate of Nakameguro Station, and turn right. Pass a large building, and take another right between the building and the Tsutaya. Walk down the shopping street until you see the cafe right in front of you.

OPENING HOURS

Monday, Thursday and Friday lunch from 11:30 to 15:30 (last order 15:00); dinner from 17:00 to 20:00. Weekends and public holidays from 11:30 to 19:00.

PRICE

1110–1650 yen for lunch and a bit more for dinner; smoothies from 600 yen; desserts from 510 yen

Rainbow Bird Rendevous
レインボーバードランデヴー

Very quiet and homely, RBR is located on a small shopping street a bit off the beaten track. The fare is simple, with staples, such as soy-meat hamburgers, comforting potato croquettes and big salads, appearing regularly along with the daily specials. The tofu steak with ginger sauce puts a great veggie twist on the popular *shogayaki*. Although the desserts change seasonally, the coffee ice-cream shake is worth a stop for an afternoon treat. They also serve a good version of vegan soft-serve ice cream, made with nuts and maple syrup. The menus are written in English, a nice surprise in such a tiny place.

Top: Try the veggie hamburger or tofu steak for a filling meal.

131

HONOURABLE MENTIONS

その他

While this guide has covered the main vegan-friendly hot spots Tokyo has to offer, here are a few more recommendations for eateries in places you might visit, but that are often skipped by visitors with limited time. Be sure to check their websites or social media before visiting, as these smaller places can have somewhat erratic hours.

KOENJI
高円寺

A bohemian area, Koenji is famous for its plethora of vintage/second-hand clothing shops, funky live music venues and long shopping streets. Koenji Station is on the Chuo Line, just four stops away from Shinjuku.

Vege & Grain Cafe Meu Nota
メウノータ

Climbing the steep little staircase and entering this retro-styled cafe feels a bit like visiting a charming version of your grandmother's attic. The reasonably priced lunch sets are filled with colour and interesting tidbits, and the 30-ingredient taco rice salad has a good punch of chilli and lots of avocado for creaminess. The curries change daily, but the chef seems to have a weakness for Sri Lankan–style concoctions.

⦿ **ADDRESS:** 2F, 3-45-11 Koenjiminami, Suginami-ku, Tokyo

KICHIJOJI
吉祥寺

Trendy and fashionable, the main draws here are Inokashira Park, a large park surrounding a lake filled with swan boats that is particularly splendid in spring and autumn, and the famous Ghibli Museum (be sure to book tickets in advance!). Kichijoji Station is on both the Chuo and Inokashira lines.

Monk's Foods
もんくすふーず

Every day, the jazz-loving owner dreams up three set menus created with seasonal ingredients, one of which is vegan. The cuisine is traditional Japanese fare based around the *ichiju sansai* (one soup and three sides) principle, so you will get three veggie dishes, miso soup and a bowl of rice. Make sure to mention you are vegan, so she gives you the correct soup. There are also a couple of other vegan spots nearby that pop up on Google Maps in case you are not in the mood for Japanese food, but check they are still open in advance, as Kichijoji is a very competitive location for restaurants and they may have closed.

📍 **ADDRESS:** 1-2-4 Gotenyama, Musashino, Tokyo

Far right: The ever-changing daily special at Nezu no Ya is always delightful.

YANAKA/NEZU/SENDAGI

谷中・根津・千駄木

These adjacent neighbourhoods are three of Tokyo's most charmingly old-school areas, with twisty, temple-lined streets and traditional wooden buildings. Check out tranquil Yanaka Cemetery, Tennoji Temple, the Yanaka Ginza shopping street and SCAI The Bathhouse. Nezu Shrine is a lovely spot with a long row of orange *torii* gates and a hill of bright azaleas that bloom from April to early May.

Yanaka can be accessed from Nippori Station on the Yamanote Line. Although walking from Yanaka to Nezu is recommended, if you are coming from a different direction Nezu Station is on the Chiyoda Line.

Nezu no Ya
根津の谷

This spritely old hand in Tokyo's vegan world has been around since 1978! The daily special is worth a gander as it changes constantly, from giant veggie-stuffed spring rolls with a nicely contrasting marinated cabbage side one early summer day, to a braised tofu and mushroom dish on a chilly winter afternoon. Since portions can be a bit modest, it is the perfect excuse to round out your meal with something sweet.

📍 **ADDRESS:** 1-1-14 Nezu, Bunkyo-ku, Tokyo

TAKADANOBABA

高田馬場

This is a major student area, thanks to nearby Waseda University. Exiting Takadanobaba Station, you will be welcomed with a colourful mural of Astro Boy. The Yayoi Kusama Museum is a short walk from nearby Waseda Station. Takadanobaba is on the Yamanote Line, just a couple of stops from Shinjuku.

Great Lakes
グレート レイクス

Home to perhaps the best vegan burgers in Tokyo, Great Lakes is a favourite among vegan expats. The caramelised onions in the 'Michigan' and complex tomato jam in the 'Ontario' elevate these burgers, which become even more decadent with an extra slice of vegan cheese. The crispy fries and shakes in limited-edition flavours like cherry chip, mint chocolate chip or black sesame are also a must. Come hungry, leave (very) happy.

📍 **ADDRESS:** 3-27-4 Nishiwaseda, Shinjuku-ku, Tokyo

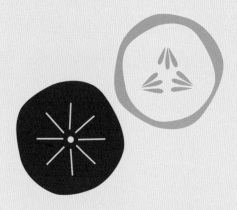

Left: You'll find some of Tokyo's finest vegan burgers at Great Lakes in Takadanobaba.

KOMAGOME
駒込

Two fine gardens are the main draw here. Rikugien is a traditional Edo-era strolling garden, and Kyu-Furukawa boasts an attractive Meiji-era Western-style residence and a combination of Japanese and European horticultural styles, including a colourful rose garden. Komagome is on the Yamanote Line, just one stop away from Sugamo and its famous 'granny shopping street', and a few stops away from major spots like Ueno, Ikebukuro and Nippori.

Nourish
ナーリッシュ

With a good selection of homely and truly delicious meals, Nourish offers lots of options. Their most famous dish is a vegan rendition of chicken *nanban*, a delightful combination of fried soy meat covered in a sweet-savoury sauce and topped with a giant dollop of homemade tartare sauce. Other satisfying standouts are the sweet and sour 'pork' and glazed *teriyaki* cutlets on a bed of fresh salad. Try the miso brownies for dessert.

⊙ **ADDRESS:** Ishikawa Kopo 2F, 1-37-8 Komagome, Toshima-ku, Tokyo

TOYOSU
豊洲

Since vegan visitors are likely to skip the tuna auctions at Toyosu Fish Market, most will travel to the man-made island of Toyosu to experience the immersive projection mapping art at teamLab Planets. Book your ticket in advance and try to visit on a weekday, if possible. There are a number of shopping malls in the area, the most interesting being Decks Tokyo Beach, where you can walk through a fun, kitschy re-creation of 1960s Japan, or stop by LEGOLAND. Toyosu Station is on the Yurakucho Line.

Vegan Ramen UZU
ヴィーガンラーメン ウズ

Projection mapping and creative ramen combine at this spot right by the famous interactive art exhibit (no ticket needed to enter this space). Try the unusual and highly photogenic green tea ramen, which has a kick of spice to balance the earthiness of the tea, or the spectacular chilled 'flower ramen', with a refreshing soup and covered in bright, edible flowers. The teas and ice cream are also quite good. Prices are high, but you are paying for the experience.

📍 **ADDRESS:** inside teamLab Planets TOKYO, 6-1-16 Toyosu, Koto-ku, Tokyo

Right: The most photogenic ramens you will ever see, served in artsy surroundings.

東京都外

FURTHER AFIELD

Now that you have plenty of ideas for where to buy awesome vegan food in Tokyo, the next question is: what about outside of the city?

If you are planning to venture out into the more rural areas of the country, then plenty of advance research (and a stash of emergency snacks) is in order. But there are lots of other, more urban destinations with vegan-friendly options.

Read on to discover some of the best day trips from the capital, as well as delicious eateries in major cities of the more southern Kansai region.

Tokyo is so expansive that you could easily spend weeks rambling around discovering all the neighbourhoods and sights. But there is far more to Japan than only its capital, and you can see a very different side of the country just by taking a day trip to a few nearby destinations.

On the pages that follow, you will find helpful tips for Yokohama, Kamakura and Saitama, chosen because they have a good selection of both easily accessible sights and vegan restaurants. But don't be afraid to venture further afield (after doing a bit of research) to spots like historical Nikko, hot spring–filled Hakone, lofty Mt. Fuji or even the far outskirts of Tokyo, like Mt. Takao or Okutama.

DAY TRIPS
FROM TOKYO

東京日帰り旅

YOKOHAMA

横浜

An easy 30 to 40-minute train ride from central Tokyo, Yokohama is a port city that was once the country's largest gateway for foreign trade. This history of exchange is still evident in the large Chinatown, former Western-style residences and attractive Meiji-period architecture.

Exit Yokohama Station, and head straight to the area around the port. Wander through the alleys of Japan's largest Chinatown, and try some delicious Chinese cuisine at Koukien, a restaurant that offers vegan options. A short walk will take you to the Motomachi area, with a lovely retro shopping street and a number of beautifully preserved Western houses on the hill in Yamate, dating back to when Japan first opened to the West. A bus or taxi ride will get you to Sankeien, a vast Japanese flower garden featuring trails dotted with historic buildings from across Japan.

Yamashita Park is on the waterfront, and is a lovely spot for a stroll to check out the Hikawa Maru ship (now a museum), elegant Hotel New Grand and slightly further afield Red Brick Warehouse. The Cup Noodles Museum is fascinating (although none of the flavours for the make-your-own experience are vegan), and the nearby Cosmoworld amusement park has a few fun rides and a huge colourful Ferris wheel.

The Shin-Yokohama Ramen Museum is a fun option for rainy days, as the interior is decked out like a Japanese town in the 1960s. There are a number of shops offering ramen in styles from all over Japan, and two of them (Ryu Shanghai Honten and Komurasaki) have vegan versions of their most famous bowls.

Koukien

好記園

Located in Chinatown, this Taiwanese restaurant is omni, but has a large selection of clearly marked vegan options. Get your fill of large *gyoza* potstickers, spicy noodles or *mapo tofu*, spring onion (scallion) pancakes and an impressive 'chicken' stir-fry. The portions are large, so if you want to try several dishes it's best to go with a group. Note that Taiwanese food tends to have more subtle flavours (although the spicy dishes have a good kick!).

⊙ **ADDRESS:** 106 Yamashitacho, Naka-ku, Yokohama

***Left:** You'll be spoilt for choice at Koukien with so many vegan options to choose from!*

Peace Cafe

ピースカフェ 横浜ジョイナス店

If you aren't in the mood for Chinese food, this reliable spot right by Yokohama Station serves up a variety of curries and sweets. The 'extreme spice' curry gets its name from the signature blend of 15 spices (rather than fieriness), and is particularly good topped with their signature tofu fried 'egg' and a crispy tofu *katsu* cutlet. Leave some room for the cacao/coffee or pumpkin pudding.

📍 **ADDRESS:** Joinus B1F, 1-5-1 Minamisaiwai, Nishi-ku, Yokohama

Left: *Get your curry fix at this friendly spot near Yokohama Station.*

M's Table
エムズ ターブル

Just a short walk from both Motomachi-Chukagai and Ishikawacho stations, this classy restaurant has a large menu with a good number of seasonal specials and gluten-free options. Their 'crispy salad pizza' is colourful and quite unique, while the soy milk–based *tantan* noodles are just the thing on a chilly day. The sauce on the bun-less soy-meat hamburger plate is complex and delivers a good punch of umami. For dessert be sure to try the rich, chestnutty soy-cream Mont Blanc, or the indulgent vegan French toast.

The chef's 2500 yen course (available at both lunch and dinner) is great value, allowing you to sample several of their specialties.

⦿ **ADDRESS:** Pompadour Building 2F, 4-171 Motomachi, Naka-ku, Kanagawa

Left: The vegan hamburgers at M's Table are delicious and covered in a decadent sauce.

KAMAKURA 鎌倉

Despite being less than 30 minutes by train from Yokohama, historic Kamakura has an entirely different feel. This small coastal city was the political centre of Japan from the late 12th to 14th century. As such, the twisty streets are lined with traditional buildings, giving visitors a little taste of the Japan of yore. The adorable Enoden tram line connects most of the major sights.

Perhaps the most iconic place to visit is the serene (and massive) Great Buddha, on the grounds of Kotokuin Temple. A short walk away is Hasedera Temple, one of the oldest in Kamakura, with great views of the coast, colourful hydrangeas in June and lots of interesting corners to explore. One fun way to experience this area is to take the Daibutsu Hiking Trail that begins near Kita-Kamakura Station, and winds through the hills, passing by Zeniarai Benzaiten Ugafuku Shrine.

There are so many temples and shrines to see that it can be hard to pick, but a few highlights are the imposing Tsurugaoka Hachimangu Shrine, the tea house in Hokokuji Temple, where you can enjoy a bowl of green tea surrounded by a bamboo grove, and pretty Meigetsuin Temple, known for its hydrangeas, autumn hues, summer irises and rabbit carvings. Take a wander along Komachi Dori street, which starts near Kamakura Station, lined with all sorts of interesting shops and eateries, many offering traditional *wagashi* sweets.

Enoshima, a little island connected to the mainland by a bridge, is also worth a look. The local shrine, pretty gardens and an observatory are all walkable, and there is a spa where you can soak in the hot springs, including one inside a cave!

Kaikoan

海光庵

Located within the grounds of Hasedera Temple, this simple restaurant offers a vegan curry and pasta dish, along with delicious fluffy steamed buns stuffed with bamboo shoots and mushrooms in a gingery sauce. The sea views make eating here extra special, and worth the entrance fee to the temple. Note that they close quite early, usually around 16:00.

📍 **ADDRESS:** 2-11-3 Hase, Kamakura

Left: The curry at Kaikoan is simple but filling.

Sorafune
穀菜カフェ　ソラフネ

Housed in a traditional wooden home, this beloved vegan eatery is about a 10-minute walk from Kamakura Station. Only open for lunch (and closed on weekends and holidays), they offer *teishoku* set meals that vary daily, along with a lighter *omusubi* rice ball option. The daily cake sets are also nice for a quick break during sightseeing.

📍 **ADDRESS:** 2-2-2 Omachi, Kamakura

Left: The daily changing teishoku *meals at Sorafune never disappoint.*

Kamakura 24sekki
カマクラ 24セッキ

About a 15-minute walk from the Great Buddha (or a slight detour off the Daibutsu Hiking Trail), this hidden gem offers sandwiches made from naturally leavened bread and filled with tempeh, vegan cutlets and local organic vegetables, along with light soups. They also have a range of both sweet and savoury baked goods and organic drinks, all served with views of the peaceful, pint-sized garden. Only open on Friday, Saturday and Sunday, and sandwiches only available until 14:00.

◉ **ADDRESS:** 923-8 Tokiwa, Kamakura, Kanagawa

Left: The sandwiches at Kamakura 24sekki taste even better with a view of the garden.

埼玉 SAITAMA

Saitama Prefecture is adjacent to Tokyo, and is often overlooked by travellers. However, it is home to a number of attractive spots, hiking trails and parks, making it an excellent break from the concrete and soaring buildings of Tokyo.

For an easy half-day trip, the retro streets of Kawagoe are a popular option. Edo-period homes and storehouses line the central area, along with cute Candy Alley. The area is known for sweet potatoes, and some of the snacks for sale are vegan (but be sure to check with staff first). Alternatively, plant lovers can head to Omiya, where the Bonsai Village and Bonsai Art Museum are the main draw.

A bit further afield in the city of Hanno, you will find Moominvalley Park and Metsä Village, a Nordic-inspired theme park celebrating Finnish author and artist Tove Jansson's Moomin characters. This is not far from the Chichibu area of Saitama, which is dotted with excellent hiking trails, Hitsujiyama Park's pink carpet of moss phlox from mid-April to early May, and farms with all-you-can-eat strawberry-picking experiences in winter and early spring.

For hikers looking to experience a more local and uncrowded trail, the 9 km (5½ mile) trek from Musashi Yokote to Koma Station (for which you can find plenty of helpful guides online) is a lovely day hike and ends close to one of Japan's veggie-friendly strongholds, the Alishan Organic Center. Kinchakuda Park right next door is particularly magical from mid-September to early October, when millions of bright-red spider lilies and fields of cosmos bloom.

Alishan Cafe
阿里山カフェ

Many a vegan in Japan owes their health and happiness to deliveries from Alishan, who have been selling veggie-friendly and organic foods since 1988. Housed in a big red barn, the cafe offers a menu that is evenly split between vegetarian and vegan options. The daily specials of miso veggie-meat or *mapo tofu* sets are always good and accompanied by plenty of fresh salad. Leave room for the indulgent carrot cake, or warm apple pie served with plant-based ice cream. After a hike on a chilly day, the warm chai also really hits the spot.

📍 **ADDRESS:** 185-2 Komahongo, Hidaka, Saitama

Above: Alishan's warm apple and fig pie is just the thing after a hike. Left: The daily specials are often very creative and include multiple smaller dishes.

While this is mainly a guide to Japan's capital, a lot of visitors travel to the more southern Kansai region, where major cities, including Kyoto, Osaka and Nara, are filled with sightseeing spots. Despite the quick *shinkansen* (bullet train) ride that puts these cities within easy reach of Tokyo, the culture, dialects and food are quite different.

Kyoto and Nara are filled with temples, shrines and streets lined with traditional wooden houses, while bustling Osaka is rather modern, as befits its role as the gateway to western Japan. From there, bullet trains can whisk you off to Hiroshima, Okayama and even Kyushu, the southernmost of the four main islands of Japan. Tiny Shikoku, the smallest main island, is most famous for the 88-temple pilgrimage that winds through its four prefectures and is a natural gem that is (for now) still under the radar.

Pro tip: make sure you stand on the right side of escalators when in Kansai, which is the opposite of Tokyo escalator etiquette!

KYOTO
& OSAKA

京都&大阪

KYOTO

京都

Kyoto is a lovely but somewhat confusing city, very much divided between the hillside areas and the flat area in the centre. Many of the most famous temples and shrines lie closer to the foot of the mountains, while the central grid is more modern, though still filled with wonderful things to discover in the side streets and covered markets.

The 'big 3' of Kyoto are Fushimi Inari Taisha Shrine, with its long winding corridors of orange *torii* gates, the strikingly golden Kinkakuji Temple (also known as the Golden Pavilion) and lofty Kiyomizudera Temple, perched on a hillside overlooking the city. However, between the city itself and nearby sights, such as green tea capital Uji, the bamboo forests of Arashiyama, the bucolic town of Kurama and (of course) nearby Nara, you could easily spend a week exploring the myriad temples, shrines and alleys lined with photogenic traditional houses.

Everyone should make their own memories and adventures in the ancient capital, but one thing I would absolutely recommend is an early morning visit to Nanzenji Temple and its incongruous aqueduct, followed by a leisurely stroll down the Philosopher's Path all the way to Kinkakuji Temple. Getting there early will allow you to miss the busloads of tourists and work up a good appetite for a hearty lunch.

Here are just a few of the vegan options in Kyoto to get you started; you'll have a great time discovering more on your own during your stay in the city of a thousand temples.

Veg Out
ベグアウト

Just across the bridge from Shichijo Station, this airy cafe has a great view of the Kamogawa River, and is only a 15-minute walk from Kyoto Station, making it a convenient spot to stop on your first or last day in town. The Veg Out plate is a good lunch option, composed of various veggie dishes that allow you to sample lots of different flavours. The gluten-free tomato coconut curry is a nice break if you are getting a bit tired of Japanese cuisine.

⊙ **ADDRESS:** Kamogawa Building 1F, 448 Inari-cho, Shimogyo-ku, Kyoto

Mumokuteki Cafe&Foods
ムモクテキ

Conveniently located a short walk from the popular Nishiki Market (and a reasonable walk from the Gion geisha district), mumokuteki offers generously portioned lunch sets and impressive desserts. A go-to is the special *gozen* set, which allows you to sample the tofu hamburger, *karaage* and *katsu* cutlet. For something a bit lighter, the *omurice* (omelette rice), made from tofu skin and covered in *demi-glace* sauce, is also a winner.

Note that their opening hours are quite short (11:30 to 17:30 on weekdays; 11:30 to 18:30 on weekends) and last order is 1 hour before closing.

⊙ **ADDRESS:** Human Forum Building 2F, 261 Shikibucho, Nakagyo-ku, Kyoto

Itadakizen
いただき繕

A 10-minute walk from Kitano Tenmangu Shrine (or 20-minute walk from Nijo Castle), Itadakizen also has branches in Sapporo, the UK and Paris. The Kyoto branch is housed within a traditional *machiya*, and serves homely favourites, such as tofu steak, a rather excellent vegan sushi roll and smooth soy-milk ramen, in a cosy atmosphere. In the evening, order a variety of side dishes and a couple of glasses of sake, perhaps with a bowl of sizzling *bibimbap* to round out dinner.

⊙ **ADDRESS:** 199-1 Nibancho, Kamigyo-ku, Kyoto

OSAKA 大阪

Quite a different experience from Kyoto, more modern Osaka is Japan's second-largest city and has a brighter, more in-your-face charm that might take a little time to get used to. Once known as 'the Nation's Kitchen', this powerhouse of the Kansai region has been a major trading port for centuries. This longstanding history linked to foodstuffs is obvious in the city itself, where colourful food stalls and restaurants with huge, eye-catching signs abound. There is even an expression that epitomises Osakians' obsession with food: *kuidaore* (eat yourself bankrupt).

Of course, there is more to the city than just its kitchens. One important spot (particularly during plum or cherry blossom season) is Osaka Castle, rising high above a massive moat surrounded by gardens and walking paths. The Dotombori shopping area is known for its Blade Runner–esque neon signs and massive restaurant shopfront decorations, which range from kraken-sized octopi to the chef's own face. Be sure to take a detour to Namba Yasaka Shrine, to pose with the huge lion head–shaped building.

The Kuromon Market, blindingly orange Sumiyoshi Taisha Grand Shrine and pretty gardens and Meiji-period buildings of Nakanoshima are also well worth a visit. And don't forget, Universal Studios Japan is also located in Osaka.

In the autumn, take a day trip to Mino'o Park and hike to magical, *daruma*-filled Katsuoji Temple to see the colours of the season.

Paprika Shokudo Vegan
パプリカ食堂

Just a short walk from the important Shinsaibashi Station, this beloved institution is a must-try. The menu is large, offering a variety of popular Japanese and Western dishes, all served in a charming, shabby-chic interior. It is hard to pick favourites, but a couple of standout dishes include the broiled 'eel' glazed with savoury-sweet *kabayaki* sauce, and the deep-fried 'oysters' made from tofu and mushrooms.

ADDRESS: 1-9-9 Shinmachi, Nishi-ku, Osaka

OKO
遊べるお好み焼き屋OKO

Another eatery near Shinsaibashi Station, this tiny, bright yellow–painted spot offers certified vegan (and gluten-free) *okonomiyaki*, one of Osaka's most loved soul foods. They also have an excellent saucy *yakisoba* (stir-fried noodles) and *gyoza*. One of the biggest selling points is the drinks menu on which everything costs just 180 yen, including alcohol, making it a cheap and cheerful place for dinner (they don't serve lunch). Chatting with the friendly owner is a big part of the fun here.

ADDRESS: 1-13-9 Higashishinsaibashi, Chuo-ku, Osaka

Neu Cat Cafe
保護ねこかふぇneu

Near Matsuyamachi Station and just a couple of stops away from Osaka Castle, this ethical cat cafe fosters kitties and kittens looking for their forever homes with great care, and is active in important TNR (Trap, Neuter and Release) operations around Osaka. The small, homely cafe is upstairs in a separate area from the cats, and offers simple and well-priced sets with plenty of veggies (and a grandmotherly slice of fruit). The fried soy meat in a sweet and spicy sauce is particularly good.

Note that it is located down a covered alleyway, so you may have to search to find it. Look for the wooden gate.

ADDRESS: 6-17-5 Tanimachi, Chuo-ku, Osaka

Helpful Hints & Tips for Visitors

While having a list of restaurants is great, there are times when you only want a quick snack or need to keep to a strict budget. Japan is a wonderfully convenient country, and the sheer variety of Tokyo's offerings means that there are several options for eating on the go or whipping up a cheap-and-cheerful impromptu picnic in your hotel or one of the city's many parks.

Please do note that because food companies do not always list every single ingredient, there is a chance that there could be a small amount of animal derivatives, amino acids or potentially even meat-based stock that is not listed on the package. While some vegans are okay with this, others are not, so if you are uncomfortable stick to non-processed foods like fruits and veggies.

CHAIN RESTAURANTS

チェーン店

Most of the chains in Tokyo will be unfamiliar to visitors, but this is of little importance as almost all of them are not good options for those with plant-based diets. Fortunately, in the run-up to the 2020 Olympics there was an increasing interest in catering to visitors and their dietary needs, so the variety has multiplied. These cheap and cheerful options can be real lifesavers if your first choice of restaurant happens to be closed.

CURRY HOUSE CoCo ICHIBANYA
カレーハウスCoCo壱番屋

This huge curry chain can be found near most large-ish train stations and purveys plates of Japanese-style curry and rice for around 500–700 yen. It is easily recognisable by the yellow and brown sign, which also shows a bowl of curry.

They offer a vegetarian curry which is free of animal products. You can add some interest to the curry and rice by selecting a few additional vegetable toppings, such as spinach, corn, eggplant (aubergine) or even the infamous *natto* (fermented soybeans). They also sometimes offer hamburgers made from soy meat as a topping as well, but be sure to double-check with staff that they're vegan.

2foods
トゥーフーズ

A newcomer to the Tokyo vegan scene, this small chain is growing fast. The menu varies a bit depending on location, but always offers reliable, 100 per cent plant-based foods, served quickly. The plant-based 'egg'–stuffed doughnut sandwich is an interesting option to try, and the spicy *mazesoba* (mixed noodles), impressive butter 'chicken' curry and melt-in-your-mouth chocolate cake are all tasty and innovative.

📍

SHIBUYA LOFT BRANCH:
Loft 2F, 21-1 Udagawacho, Shibuya-ku, Tokyo

TOKYO STATION BRANCH:
Yaesu Shopping Mall (underground) North-1, 2-1 Yaesu, Chuo-ku, Tokyo

GINZA LOFT BRANCH: Loft 1F, 2-4-6 Ginza, Chuo-ku, Tokyo

ARK HILLS BRANCH: Karajan Square, Ark Towers West, 1-3-40 Roppongi, Minato-ku, Tokyo

AZABU JUBAN BRANCH:
3-11-3 Motoazabu, Minato-ku, Tokyo

OMOTESANDO BRANCH:
Sepia Harajuku 1F,
4-5-12 Jingumae,
Shibuya-ku, Tokyo

**SHINJUKU MYLORD
BRANCH:** Mosaic Street,
1-1-3 Nishishinjuku,
Shinjuku-ku, Tokyo

HIBIYA BRANCH: Tokyo
Midtown Hibiya B1F,
1-1-2 Yuraku-cho,
Chiyoda-ku, Tokyo

EBISU BRANCH: Atre Ebisu
6F, 1-5-5 Ebisuminami,
Shibuya-ku, Tokyo

**KOMAZAWA OLYMPIC
PARK BRANCH:**
1-1-2 Komazawakoen,
Setagaya-ku, Tokyo

Mr. FARMER
ミスターファーマー

There are five branches of the farm-to-table
Mr. FARMER around Tokyo, and one in Yokohama.
As the menu is based around West Coast health-
food favourites, the vegan options tend to lean
towards veggie burgers, soups, rice bowls and
salads. The desserts are usually vegan and often
include a gluten-free option, with fresh tarts and
cakes available at most branches. While staff may
not speak English, the menus make it clear which
items are vegan, gluten-free and even low carb!
Do keep in mind that the prices are on par with the
trendiness of the restaurants.

*The salad bowls at Mr. FARMER
are generously portioned and
served with your choice of
homemade dressing.*

Far East Bazaar
ファーイーストバザール

This Arabian Nights–inspired chain has four shops inside fancy department stores in Tokyo (with those in Shibuya's Hikarie and Shinjuku's Lumine 1 being the easiest to access), along with two outposts in Osaka, and one each in Kyoto, Nagoya and Hiroshima. You can buy all sorts of interesting dried fruits here, but the real draw is the vegan ice-cream sandwiches. Sample interesting flavours, such as pistachio, fig or date and chocolate, pressed between two crispy cookies made from ancient grains. The company also has a beautiful restaurant – Carvaan Tokyo – in Shibuya, where they offer a selection of vegan Middle Eastern and Mediterranean dishes.

The selection of vegan ice-cream sandwiches is reason enough to visit one of Far East Bazaar's eateries.

OTHER VEGAN OPTIONS

他のオプション

When hunger suddenly strikes, it can be tough to stop exploring and go find a restaurant, or you may want to save some cash by having some meals at your accommodation. No worries, this section has got you covered!

Navigating Japanese convenience stores, supermarkets and other shops can be a bit daunting, but follow these tips to make it smoother. And when in doubt, ask for help! The staff may not speak English, but using translation apps and simple words, you often can get your question across.

CONVENIENCE STORES
コンビニ

Finding a *conbini* (convenience store) in Japanese cities is rarely an issue, and sometimes it seems like there is one on every street corner. But the best option for vegan and gluten-free snacks is Natural Lawson, a fancier and supposedly more health-conscious version of the ubiquitous Lawson chain.

These stores always have a stock of vegan and gluten-free bars, some of which indicate this on the packaging in English, as well as a selection of macrobiotic cookies made by Biokura and Chaya Macrobiotics. Along with fresh-cut fruit, dried fruit, nuts and even a small selection of gluten-free bread produced by Maisen, this is the easiest and most reliable spot to find something to munch on. The chilled section usually has a good stock of soy milk, sometimes in seasonal flavours, along with oat and almond milks and pre-packaged fruit and veggie smoothies. There will often be individual packets of tofu and some of the *onigiri* rice balls are also safe and have a bit of English on the package. Make sure to check the cup noodle section to see if they have T's Tantan ramen, which is both vegan and delicious. The stock does change, so take some time to explore the racks and see what goodies are available. With more than 120 stores located in key parts of Tokyo alone, you are sure to come across one at least a few times during your visit.

Other convenience stores, such as 7-11, FamilyMart, Sunkus and Circle K, have varying degrees of English-language signage, so can be a bit of an adventure. A reliable standby in most cases will be the *ume* (pickled plum), *sekihan* (a reddish mixture of rice and adzuki beans) or plain salt *onigiri*. *Inari sushi*, sweetened fried tofu pouches stuffed with rice, may look vegan, but they are usually soaked in fish broth. Soy milk is commonly available and generally located by the juice boxes. Pickled veggies, single-serve tofu sets, salted *edamame* and simple packaged salads are also easy to find.

SUPERMARKETS
スーパー

Japanese supermarkets can be beguiling, but the almost complete lack of English and unhelpful packaging make them a bit intimidating.

Much like convenience stores, simple prepared foods, such as cut fruit, salads and rice balls, as well as microwavable packs of rice, are quite common. In the deli section there will be a lot of animal-based foods, but products like salted *edamame*, pickles and noodles – without the sauce, which is sure to contain fish – are available in most stores. Tofu is abundant and absolutely delicious, even when just topped with a drizzle of soy sauce or salt. Keep your eye out for *goma dofu*, little packs of black sesame tofu often stocked in the same area as regular tofu, which is wonderfully rich and hard to find outside of Japan.

In the dairy section you can find soy milk: look for the characters 豆乳. Do take notice of the colour of the packaging: the green ones are processed (and so taste a bit smoother and sweeter), while the brown ones are unsweetened and taste quite strongly of beans. Almond and oat milks have also become more common. There is a brand of soy yoghurt, unfortunately only available in large containers, produced by Marusan. You may see smaller pots of soy yoghurt produced by Soyafarm, but they contain gelatine so are best avoided.

While they look very tempting, breads in supermarkets should be skipped, as they are almost invariably not vegan.

SPECIALTY STORES
専門店

Just as in any large city, Tokyo has a large population of consumers who want safe, organic health food, supplements and supplies. There are a couple of smaller organic grocers (such as the store attached to Nezu no Ya), as well as some larger suppliers.

A new option that has popped up in the past few years is the French organic supermarket chain Bio c' Bon, which has 28 branches (and counting) spread across Tokyo and neighbouring Kanagawa Prefecture. Most of their stock is imported, with many European brands available. They generally have a good (if pricey) range of vegan-friendly snacks, sweets, frozen foods, plant milks and other basics. The Harajuku, Ginza and Nakameguro branches are easy to stop by for a browse while sightseeing.

Another small chain is Natural House. While the main store in Omotesando has an eat-in space, most of the other branches are smaller and usually located inside department stores. They have a small selection of vegan, gluten-free and allergen-free options, varying from curries to desserts, but unfortunately much of the packaging is often only in Japanese. Just take the product you wish to buy to the staff and show them the vegan card included in this guide. They will be happy to double-check for you.

Keep your eye out for branches of Cosme Kitchen and Biople, found in most major cities across Japan. They offer a small selection of cruelty-free beauty products, along with some vegan-friendly snacks and drinks. National chains Kaldi and Carnival also have some imported vegan snacks, as do high-end supermarkets like Queen's Isetan, Seijo Ishii and BIO-RAL.

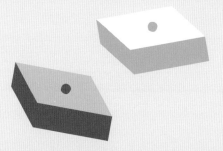

COFFEE CHAINS
コーヒー屋

Tokyo runs on coffee, so you will find plenty of coffee and tea chains around the city. As usual, Starbucks is very good at serving the vegan community, as most drinks can be switched to soy, almond or oat milk. Staff members are also usually careful to ask about whipped cream and other additions, making it a stress-free experience. While the coffee is pretty much the same all over the world, the matcha latte (green tea latte) is made using much higher quality tea, so is a must-try as an alternative to your morning cup of Arabica. Another only-in-Japan item is the rather addictive *hojicha* latte, made with roasted green tea which gives off a deep, slightly smoky aroma.

The Seattle-based chain Tully's and local Doutor coffee shops have soy milk–based coffee and tea drinks, but be careful about more fanciful options, as there may be some condensed milk or honey lurking in your cup. Tully's also offers two plant-based meals: a somewhat unique lasagna and a taco rice bowl.

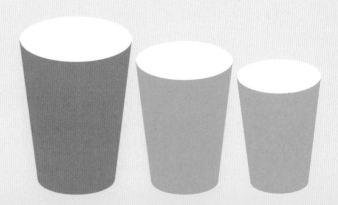

FARMERS' MARKETS & FESTIVALS
ファーマーズマーケットとフェスティバル

Tokyo hosts several vegan and health food–oriented festivals and markets each year, but the two below are your best bet for quality and fun value.

Farmer's Market @UNU
ファーマーズマーケット@UNU

📍 **ADDRESS**
5-53-70 Jingumae, Shibuya-ku, Tokyo (in front of the United Nations University)

🚩 **HOW TO GET THERE**
from Exit B2 of Omotesando Station, walk straight for about 5 minutes until you reach an intersection. The market will be on your right.

🕐 **OPENING HOURS**
Saturday–Sunday from 10:00 to 16:00

If you want organic veggies, hand-pressed juices, artisan bread or pretty crafts, make sure to stop by this longstanding farmers' market. While the stalls change weekly, you are almost certain to find at least a couple of purveyors of vegan baked goods and some food trucks with plant-based dishes. Keep an eye out for Terra Burgers and Go Muffins Go in particular.

Vegan Gourmet Festival
ビーガングルメ祭り

📍 **ADDRESS**
Kiba Park

🚩 **HOW TO GET THERE**
turn left out of Exit 1 of Kiba Station and walk straight until you see the park entrance.

🕐 **OPENING HOURS**
check online as exact dates vary

While this event is excellent, attracting vegan stalls from across the country to beautiful Kiba Park, the organisers rarely publish information in English, so your best bet is to check their Instagram (@veganfesoffice) for updates. They have previously held events in Kyoto and Nagoya as well.

USEFUL JAPANESE WORDS & PHRASES

役立ち単語集

All the businesses in this guide are vegan-friendly and have a decent understanding of dietary restrictions. However, non vegan–specific restaurants and shops may require a little more effort. While many eateries in Japan are trying to improve the level of English they offer (by either producing translated menus or hiring employees with language skills), it is still helpful to have a bit of backup.

If you want to ask if a dish contains animal products or allergens:

Does this contain … ?

… は入っていますか … wa haitte imasuka?

English	Japanese	Pronunciation
meat	肉	niku
fish	魚	sakana
shellfish	魚介	gyokai
milk products	乳製品	nyuuseihin
eggs	卵	tamago
egg white	卵白	ranpaku
honey	ハチミツ	hachimitsu
beef	牛肉	gyuuniku
pork	豚肉	butaniku
chicken	鶏肉	toriniku
animal-based extracts	動物性エキス	doubutsusei ekisu
fish flakes	かつお節	katsuobushi
wheat	小麦	komugi
gluten	でん粉	denpun
alcohol	アルコール	arukooru

If shopping or asking for substitutions, the following may prove helpful:

Excuse me, do you have ... ?

すみません、... ありますか

Sumimasen, ... arimasu ka?

If you wish to ask to have a particular ingredient removed or left out, then use the phrase below.

Without ... please.

...抜きお願いします。

...nuki onegaishimasu.

You can insert the words listed on page 173 as needed, or more specific terms. Be aware that snippets of cheese, ham, bacon and fish flakes tend to get sprinkled over a lot of dishes, so it is always good to check with the staff before ordering. English words, such as cheese, bacon and ham, are also used in Japanese; just make sure to speak slowly for non-English speakers.

As always when travelling around a foreign country, make sure to be upbeat and polite when asking staff for alterations. Causing a scene or being aggressive in Japan is definitely frowned upon, and a smile and multiple thank yous are much more likely to get you what you want.

FINALLY ...

I truly hope that this guide helps you enjoy the culinary delights of my beloved Tokyo and that you leave with great memories, cherished photos and an appreciation for vegan Japanese cuisine. I would love to hear from you at @tokyoveganguide or the #tokyoveganguide tag on Instagram.

Did you find that a restaurant has closed or changed their menu completely? If so, I apologise in advance. The editorial team and I did our very best to ensure that all the restaurants, shops and other services mentioned were open and in business before going to print.

And finally, thank you for purchasing my book and for choosing to live a little lighter and with more compassion towards our fellow creatures.

ACKNOWLEDGEMENTS

After years of self-publishing my vegan guides to Tokyo, becoming a published author is a long-held dream that finally came true. I have the deepest appreciation for the Smith Street Books team, who helped make this guide the best it can be. Particular thanks go to Lucy Heaver, editor extraordinaire, Gorta Yuuki who took the beautiful photos and Michelle Mackintosh for the gorgeous design work.

Special thanks to Tatsuro, who ate far more than his fair share of brown rice while I researched Tokyo's vegan restaurants, and my parents, the first reviewers of the guide, who have always been supportive of my choice to be plant-based. And a big hug to Lupin, our rescue kitty, who sat on my lap for hours as I feverishly wrote to meet the deadline.

ABOUT THE AUTHOR

Chiara's connection with Japan began around 2007, and she has been a Tokyo resident since 2011. A creative jack-of-all-trades, she is a writer/editor, tourism consultant, singer, narrator and anchor for a Japanese language program on NHK, Japan's national broadcaster.

Chiara spends a good deal of time exploring remote areas of Japan, looking for vegan-friendly local foods, coffee and a place to plug in her laptop. She was inspired to write *The Vegan Guide to Tokyo* to help veggie visitors to Japan's capital find meals worthy of travelling across the ocean for. Feel free to follow her never-ending quest for great vegan food on Instagram at @tokyoveganguide.

Published in 2023 by Smith Street Books
Naarm (Melbourne) | Australia
smithstreetbooks.com

ISBN: 978-1-9227-5419-6

Publisher: Paul McNally
Editor: Lucy Heaver, Tusk studio
Designer: Michelle Mackintosh
Design layout: Megan Ellis
Photographer: Gorta Yuuki
Proofreader: Eugenie Baulch

Printed & bound in China
by C&C Offset Printing Co., Ltd.

Book 257
10 9 8 7 6 5 4 3 2 1